"From the first time I heard Fr. Khaled's preaching, I always wanted to be able to savor this gift and return to his words. It is a delight that these homilies are appearing in print at last. The voice within these pages addresses needs of our times with pastoral sensitivity and situational particularity, ordered by the liturgical rhythm of the Byzantine church. At the same time, the homilies are composed with a deep, sonorous familiarity with Scripture as a way of thinking, speaking, and living in intimacy with Christ through the Holy Spirit in the sight of the Father. Their distinctive grace is at once to echo and to renew the patristic tradition; they offer a model for prayerful expression of godly love within a modern ecumenical ecclesia."

—JANE HEATH
Durham University

"In our broken world, in the midst of personal sin and social sin, in the midst of suffering and death, we need salvation. But even many Christians—all too often including myself—have forgotten what 'salvation' might mean, beyond the simple desire for health and prosperity. What Fr. Anatolios does in these sermons is to reintroduce, step by step, what salvation in Christ is and why it is the pearl of great price. These beneficent sermons are an invitation to enter into the kingdom of Christ, the kingdom of salvation, here and now."

—MATTHEW LEVERING
Mundelein Seminary

T0006341

"This volume of sermons on the major feasts of the Byzantine liturgical tradition is itself a feast of words that will nourish and sustain any readers fortunate enough to enjoy its bounties, whether they are pastors looking to serve a richer banquet to their hungry congregations or lay people eager for greater sustenance in an increasingly undernourished world. Each homily reflects a rare ability to tie the scriptural message not only to the liturgical moment but also to patristic theology and to the larger life of Christian discipleship. The sermons represent the triumph of showing how the patristic model of preaching offers a valuable mode of speaking to modern believers."

—GEORGE PARSENIOS
Holy Cross Greek Orthodox School of Theology

Feasts for the Kingdom

Sermons for the Liturgical Year

Khaled Anatolios

William B. Eerdmans Publishing Company

Grand Rapids, Michigan

Wm. B. Eerdmans Publishing Co.
4035 Park East Court SE, Grand Rapids, Michigan 49546
www.eerdmans.com

29 28 27 26 25 24 23   1 2 3 4 5 6 7

ISBN 978-0-8028-8303-2

Library of Congress Cataloging-in-Publication Data

A catalog record for this book is available from the Library of
Congress.

For Rebecca and Sarah,
judicious and benevolent critics of their father's sermons

CONTENTS

CHRISTMAS SEASON

THEOPHANY

LENT, PART 1

FEAST OF THE ANNUNCIATION

LENT, PART 2

PALM SUNDAY

GREAT AND HOLY FRIDAY

EASTER VIGIL

EASTER SEASON

SUNDAY OF THE MYRRH-BEARING WOMEN

ASCENSION

PENTECOST

TRANSFIGURATION

FOREWORD

Readers of these sermons will discover that they are indeed "sermons for the liturgical year," but not quite in the way Western Christians expect. Anatolios is a Byzantine Catholic— an Eastern Catholic—and his church year is the Byzantine one that begins not in late November with Advent texts of Jesus's expected arrival but in early September with texts of Jesus's inaugural preaching. Further, his sermons are for the "*Feasts* of the Kingdom," for example, the Easter feast, the Ascension feast, the Pentecost feast. Commemoration of these events is for him not merely a remembrance but a festive celebration, and preaching about them is complete only with the Eucharist that follows—an anticipation of the Heavenly Banquet.

I find the sermons in this collection deeply nourishing. They are themselves feasts for the soul. So many of us have heard or read sermons in which the preacher appears to think they must supply electrical current to get those old Scriptures to come alive. Maybe the preacher will offer cute stories, or turn the sermon into the preacher's Facebook page, or promise believers that their faith should get them a boatload of cash.

You will find nothing like that here. Father Anatolios trusts God's Word to have its own power. He never tries to add his own juice to it. He always connects us to the power that is already there. To preach like this requires integrity and faith. The author believes that if Matthew, Mark, and Luke were good enough for the Holy Spirit to inspire, then they're good enough to inspire us. If the Bible's story is of the incarnation of the eternal Son of God, of his atoning death and victorious resurrection, of his ascension to the right hand of God the Father, of the Holy Spirit poured out by the Father and the Son, then who are we to tell a different story, or our own little stories, or baggage of some other kind?

Trust the Bible to have its own power.

What follows for Fr. Anatolios is that Christian sermons ought to be relentlessly Christ-centered. Accordingly, in these pages you will read that our world is always old, but Jesus's love is always new. That we human beings are stooped over from the weight of our sin, but Jesus lifts our burden so we may stand straight and tall and free. That though we are a failed human race in so many ways, nonetheless—through the hospitality of the Virgin—we gave birth to God!

In the Apostles' Creed we confess our faith in "Jesus Christ, God's only Son, our Lord." The creed then goes on to recite the events of Christ—his conception by the Holy Spirit and birth from the Virgin Mary; his suffering, crucifixion, death, and burial; his resurrection, ascension, and session at the right hand of God. In many ways, Fr. Anatolios simply follows the creed along as he preaches, plumbing Christ's events at their depths and drawing up their significance for our faith and sustenance. His intention is clear.

Preach *Christian* sermons that center on Jesus Christ.

Finally, the sermons in this collection do what all good sermons should do. They awaken the heart to say Yes! to God and the good and No! to the devil and evil.

"True religion," said Jonathan Edwards, "consists in great measure in . . . the fervent exercises of the heart."* Edwards meant that, at its core, true religion has to do not just with kindling our passions but also with aiming them in the right direction. The world is full of good. The godly person must say Yes! to it with all their heart and then act accordingly. The world is also full of evil. The godly person must say No! to it with all their heart and then act accordingly. The world is full of the mixture of good and evil so that the godly person sometimes needs the gift of discernment before they *know* what to say or how to act.

In any event, true religion always begins from the central place in us where we "hate what is evil" and "hold fast to what is good" (Rom. 12:9). A sequence of hearty Yes's and No's lies at the center of true religion, said Edwards, and this is why we sing our praise instead of merely saying it. This is why we preach the word instead of simply reading it. This is why in the Lord's Supper we "eat and drink our God."**

The reason in each case is that we want God to get our hearts going again, and we want the passions of our hearts to find their true target. For example, we want love and joy to start up, and we especially want these "affections," as Edwards called them, to be aimed at God. We want the reality of God to be big enough to see with the eyes of faith and good enough to taste with the mouth of faith. To "taste and

---

* Jonathan Edwards, *Religious Affections* (1746), ed. John E. Smith (New Haven: Yale University Press, 1959), 99.

** Edwards, *Religious Affections*, 115.

see that the Lord is good" (Ps. 34:8) meant for Edwards that we need preaching and the sacraments to give us a sense of God's "sweetness" and "glorious brightness."*

I can pay Fr. Anatolios's sermons no higher tribute than to say that they do what Edwards prescribed. These sermons, with their passion and forthrightness and deep presentation of Scripture, move the heart, often powerfully. They provoke and then assure the heart. They stir and settle and then stir the heart again. No gimmicks here. Just a simple and noble strategy:

- Trust the Bible to have its own power.
- Preach *Christian* sermons that center on Jesus Christ.
- Expect the Holy Spirit to move the hearts of faithful believers.

Fr. Anatolios follows a winning recipe. The reason I think so is that his sermons let me "taste and see that the Lord is good."

Cornelius Plantinga

---

* Edwards, *Religious Affections*, 95.

PREFACE

I believe that there are as many ways to proclaim the Word
of God as there are individual persons entrusted with the
gift and responsibility to fulfill that task. Each person
brings their own story, their own abilities and disabilities, into their human collaboration with the Holy Spirit
in the proclamation of the Word. In the end, the content
of our abilities and disabilities matters less than openness
to the Spirit, which purifies and elevates our human ca-
pacities, "heals our infirmities, and compensates for our
deficiencies."*

The homilies collected in this volume bear the stamp
of the story of my own conversion to Christian faith.
Having grown up Muslim, I converted to Christianity as
a young adult. The initial impetus for my conversion was
the reading of the New Testament, which I had put on a
list of great works of fiction that I endeavored to read as

* This phrase is from one of the prayers in the Byzantine liturgy for
the ordination of priests.

part of my self-imposed training as an aspiring novelist. Once I decided to become a Christian, on the basis of my newfound conviction that the New Testament was in fact nonfiction, I became aware of the need to learn more about how the contents of the New Testament could be translated into a way of life and an interpretation of the ultimate meaning of reality. At that time, I had no affiliation or contact with any Christian community. Instead, I went to the local library in Victoria, British Columbia, where I lived at the time, to find books about Christianity. At first, I was delighted to discover that there were even more gospels than the ones in my little New Testament book, such as the Gospel of Thomas, for example! Though at the time, I had no inkling of the notion of "Gnosticism" or the distinction between "canon" and "apocrypha," the overall ambience of these "gospels" struck me as being closer to my original estimation of the New Testament as fiction.* They seemed to exude an altogether different air, more exotic but less vital, than that of the canonical gospels. But then I found, in the same area of the library, St. Augustine's *City of God*. This was an altogether different genre than the New Testament, and yet I sensed a deep kinship of spirit between the two texts. Thus began my still-continuing endeavor to learn to live the Christian faith under the guidance of the fathers of the church and their contemplation of Scripture. I began to learn what it meant to be a Christian primarily from reading the church fathers and, as a scholar of early Christian theology, I am still continuing that learning.

---

* The apocryphal "gospels" I found in the library were accounts of Jesus that were not accepted by the church as inspired testimonies to its faith in Jesus as Lord. A number of these "gospels" originated among sectarian communities that came to be known in the Christian tradition as "gnostic."

These homilies also continue that learning and apply it to the ministry of the liturgical proclamation of the Word. When I was ordained a priest and tasked with the ministry of preaching, six years ago at the time of this writing, I naturally and without conscious deliberation executed that task in what I took to be the style and approach of the fathers. I note this fact not to insinuate any claim of equality in either quality or authority between these homilies and the work of the fathers, but only to acknowledge some of the ways in which these homilies depart from the customary modern styles of preaching. Among these elements of variance with contemporary approaches, which are ascribable partly or wholly to my reflexive aspiration for an affinity with patristic approaches to reading, praying, and proclaiming Scripture, two are especially worthy of note from the outset: the primacy of the language world of the Bible, and the all-encompassing centrality of Trinitarian and christological doctrine.

To speak specifically of the primacy of biblical language and not just of the authority or inerrancy of biblical teaching is to acknowledge that the very words of Scripture mediate a salvific encounter with God. A direct consequence of this principle is that such a salvific encounter is realized, from the human side, not by making targeted expeditions to extract "lessons" for life and faith but rather by letting biblical language structure one's thoughts and feelings. The Scriptures are not merely a storehouse of a list of doctrines but the "green pastures" in which we are *Ps. 23* meant to repose for the salvific healing and refreshment of our hearts and minds. Applied to scriptural meditation, this principle dictates that the reader, under the guidance of the Holy Spirit, should use the assigned scriptural readings as a springboard for making links with other scriptural texts, linking Scripture to Scripture, and thus interpreting Scripture by Scripture. In this way, the "sufficiency" of Scripture (Athanasius),* as constituting its own world of meaning through which our own lives find their true meaning, is achieved.

The fathers of the church also taught me that the key that opens up the Scriptures, and the center that pervades the circumference of the scriptural world, is the recognition of the risen Lord, in the power of the Spirit, as the

Heb. 1:3   eternal "radiance" of the Father's glory. Scriptural meditation, whether in the mode of private prayer or preaching, does not achieve integrity without this reference to Christ and to Christ's revelation of God as Father, Son, and Holy Spirit. Acceptance of this principle does not mean that every scriptural meditation must include a conscious review of the fine details of the church's formulation of Trinitarian and christological doctrines. But it does mean that every reading of Scripture must strive to be a reading in the Holy Spirit that also invokes the Spirit, and a recognition of Christ as the eternally beloved Son who speaks only the

John 12:49   words of the Father and of whom the Father says, "Listen
Matt. 17:5   to him." Readers of these homilies will not generally find in them expositions of Trinitarian and christological doctrine. But they will find indications of the habit of reading Scripture in a Trinitarian-christological key, a habit in which I was trained through my study of the fathers.

I hope it is not true, however, that these homilies are merely contrived imitations of the "style" of the fathers. It is true enough that I learned to read the Scriptures under the guidance of the fathers, but when I read the Scriptures, whether for my private prayer or for the sake of proclaim-

---

* Athanasius, *Against the Greeks* 1.

ing the Word as a minister of Christ, I am trying to hear
the voice of Christ himself, the only true Teacher, not to
remember what the church fathers said. Readers of these
homilies will note that I almost never quote the fathers
directly. Moreover, while indeed Christ himself is "the
same yesterday, today, and forever," it is also true that the   *Heb. 13:8*
voice of Christ speaks to us, in the Spirit, in the midst of
our very particular and unique situations and transforms
these situations from within. For the most part, these
homilies were prayed over, composed, and preached in
the midst of the Covid pandemic and great political and
social unrest, and they are efforts to hear and communi-
cate the voice of Christ in these very specific contexts. In
terms of their objective and explicit content, these homilies are much more preoccupied with this living context
than with "what the fathers said."

A final oddity of these homilies that requires a word
of explanation for many readers is their adherence to
the Byzantine liturgical calendar. I am a priest of the
Melkite Greek Catholic Church, a church that has its
historical origins in the Arabic-speaking Middle East
and that follows the liturgical and spiritual practices of
the Byzantine tradition while maintaining eucharistic
communion with the Roman Catholic Church. These
homilies follow the Byzantine liturgical calendar and
reflect on the scriptural readings prescribed therein. At
the same time, I believe that the two overarching commitments I noted above—to the primacy of scriptural
language and to the centrality of the Trinitarian and
christological mysteries of Christian faith—constitute
a bridge between the particularities of the Byzantine
liturgical tradition and the common faith of those who
confess Jesus Christ as Lord and Savior.

May the readers of these homilies find in them motivation and encouragement to dedicate themselves wholly to the confession of the lordship of Christ, in word and deed, in the power and overflowing love of the Holy Spirit, to the glory of God our Father.

ACKNOWLEDGMENTS

The homilies collected in this volume are the fruit of my ministry with the Byzantine Catholic community at the University of Notre Dame. I was commissioned to this ministry by Bishop Nicholas Samra, who at that time was Melkite Greek Catholic bishop of the United States. My first thanks go to him for initially inviting me to consider a call to the priesthood and for supporting and nurturing my priestly ministry. It was Bishop Nicholas who encouraged me to initiate the offering of the Byzantine Divine Liturgy at the University of Notre Dame, beginning in 2015. His stated goal for this mission was that the Catholic Church at Notre Dame might be fully Catholic in its embrace of both the Eastern and Western trajectories of the Catholic tradition and may be enabled thus to "breathe with both lungs," in the famous words of St. John Paul II. The Byzantine Catholic community at Notre Dame owes a foundational debt of gratitude to Bishop Nicholas for all the fruits of our worship and witness at Notre Dame, among which are these homilies.

At the same time, this commissioning by an Eastern Catholic bishop would have been to no avail were it not for the warm and encouraging hospitality of the President of Notre Dame, Fr. John Jenkins, CSC, and of the local Roman Catholic bishop, Kevin Rhoades. Bishop Rhoades has welcomed and embraced our presence at Notre Dame and has made a habit of celebrating with us at our liturgies on a regular basis, while Fr. Jenkins has been a reliable source of encouragement and support since my first days at Notre Dame and the first beginnings of this ministry. I am happy to have this occasion to express publicly my gratitude to them, as well as to Fr. Pete McCormick, head of Campus Ministry at Notre Dame, who has been a constant source of creative solicitude for the needs of our Byzantine Catholic community at Notre Dame.

Every self-aware preacher knows how much the prayers and witness of the worshipping assembly are crucially instrumental in calling forth the preacher's homiletic mediation of God's Word. I have known and felt that hidden spiritual collaboration throughout my ministry with the Byzantine Catholic community at Notre Dame and I am deeply thankful to all of those who have prayed with us over the years. I would be remiss if I did not express my thanks also to all the members of Our Lady of the Annunciation Melkite Catholic Cathedral in Boston, who were my first trainers and guardians in the ministry of priesthood. In particular, this collection of homilies was called forth by the encouragement of particular people who encouraged me to share these sermons more publicly, among whom I owe special thanks to Nathan and Jessie Eubank, Jane Heath, Mary Kerby, Francesca Murphy, and Sr. Mary Riccé. Throughout the publication process, I have greatly benefited from the creative and discerning collaboration of James Ernest, vice president and editor in chief at Eerdmans, and also from the meticulous, prompt, and insightful guidance of Jenny Hoffman and the editorial staff at Eerdmans. I am happy to invite readers of this book, who are the beneficiaries of their diligent labors, to share in my gratitude to them.

Of course, in everything I do as a priest, my greatest human debt of gratitude goes to my faithful collaborator in this ministry, Presbytera Meredith, my wife. In the case of these homilies, an equal debt of thanks goes to my two youngest children, Rebecca and Sarah. Typically, our trip back from church begins with Rebecca proclaiming from the back of the car, "Homily feedback time!" After which ensues a spirited offering of evaluative comments that are insightful and lovingly supportive, sometimes delicately intermingled with discreet euphemistic critique. I dedicate this book to Sarah and Rebecca, with the fervent hope that the Word of God may continue to dwell in them richly as they teach and admonish me in these and other *Col. 3:16* matters and that the Holy Spirit may sustain them and nurture them into the "measure of the stature of the full- *Eph. 4:13* ness of Christ."

BYZANTINE LITURGICAL NEW YEAR

CHRIST, OUR TODAY

1 Timothy 2:1–7; Luke 4:16–22

My brothers and sisters who are dearly beloved in Christ Jesus our Lord:

It is an especially fitting grace that our first celebration of the Byzantine liturgy in this new academic year happens to fall on the first day of the Byzantine liturgical year. As many of you know, the Western liturgical calendar begins with Advent. But the Byzantine liturgical calendar begins today, on September 1, which is a custom that reflects the practice of the ancient Byzantine empire of beginning the civil year in September.

There is a nice complementarity between these two different beginnings of the liturgical year in East and West. The Western calendar wants us to make a new beginning every year by awaiting the birth of Christ and the renewal of the grace of Emmanuel, God-with-us, in our lives. Now, I suppose that we could see the Eastern calendar as simply conforming itself to the secular calendar of its time. But it would be more charitable, and ultimately truer, to understand it as inviting us to convert the rhythm of our secular time into sacred time, into Christ-time.

Of course, it is no longer true that the secular year begins for us on September 1. But, for most of us who are associated in one way or another with school, at different levels, the beginning of the academic year around this time is really the more significant beginning of a new year than January 1.

As we begin a new academic year, we have our plans, our goals and ambitions, our anxieties and worries about the coming year. But, today, we are invited to recognize that none of these goals and ambitions and anxieties and worries is of any real significance at all, apart from the one thing needful: to know Jesus Christ, to enter into his kingdom, to be immersed into his death, to live each day out of the life of his resurrection, to be filled with his Spirit. And all of this is available for us, without cost and without limit, through the Divine Liturgy.

Today's gospel anchors the beginning of the liturgical year in the beginning of Jesus's public ministry. Jesus enters into the synagogue to celebrate the liturgy on the Sabbath, and he reads from the Scriptures, and he declares to the people that these Scriptures are now fulfilled in him. He is the one who has been anointed and filled with God's Spirit, the one who has been sent to bring good news to the poor, to proclaim liberty to the captives, and recovery of sight to

Luke 4:14–19   the blind, to proclaim the year of the Lord's favor.

How wonderful it must have been to be present at that synagogue when Jesus said these words in the flesh. The gospel tells us that "the eyes of all in the synagogue were

Luke 4:20   fixed on him," and they were amazed at the gracious words

Luke 4:22   that came from his mouth. But, in fact, things are no different for us. Today, we are invited to recognize that the mission of Jesus, which he proclaimed to the people in that synagogue, still continues at every celebration of the Divine Liturgy, throughout the liturgical year.

Whenever we celebrate the Divine Liturgy, the risen Jesus is present and he is the real celebrant of this liturgy. At every liturgy, he says to us: "The Spirit of God is upon me. Come and be filled with my Spirit and out of my heart shall flow rivers of living water for you to drink from." At every liturgy, the risen Lord continues his mission of proclaiming good news to the poor—the ultimate good news that he replaces the poverty of our humanity with the riches of his divinity (see 2 Cor. 8:9), the good news that he addresses first of all to those who struggle with every form of material poverty. Whenever we celebrate the Divine Liturgy and to the extent that we live within the flow of liturgical time, the risen Jesus proclaims to us freedom from captivity, the captivity of a merely worldly existence. A merely worldly existence, after all, is a terrible prison for the human spirit that is destined to enjoy the freedom of the glory of being children of God and partakers of the divine nature. Whenever we celebrate the Divine Liturgy, Jesus takes away the blindness of our seeing the world without the eyes of the gospel and enables us to have our eyes always fixed on him—as the gospel tells us that "the eyes of all in the synagogue were fixed on him."

My brothers and sisters, this first day of the liturgical year is a kind of feast of the renewal of our covenant with God, the new covenant of the crucified and risen Lord, the one Mediator between God and humanity. On this day, the risen Lord promises to accompany us in the days ahead, to enfold all our coming days, with all their joys and sorrows, into the everlasting *Today* of the fullness of his presence.

We enter into this everlasting *Today*, this fullness of time, whenever we celebrate the Divine Liturgy. Whenever we celebrate the Divine Liturgy, Jesus proclaims to us: "Today this Scripture has been fulfilled in your hear-

Luke 4:18

John 7:38

2 Cor. 8:9

Luke 4:18

Rom. 8:21

2 Pet. 1:4

Luke 4:18

Luke 4:20

1 Tim. 2:5

Luke 4:21

ing." Whenever we celebrate the Divine Liturgy, the risen Lord promises us unfailing and complete fulfillment, the fulfillment of being filled with the one in whom the fullness of God dwells bodily, the one who is the fulfillment of everything we desire and much more than we know how to desire.

Col. 2:9

So, my brothers and sisters, let us now recommit ourselves to our part of this covenant, which is simply to live our coming days in the *Today* of Jesus Christ, to convert our secular time to sacred time, to live our whole lives out of the Divine Liturgy and into the Divine Liturgy, to always have our eyes fixed on Jesus, and to always be amazed at the gracious words that come out of his mouth and, of course, to be doers of his word and not hearers only.

James 1:22

Let us now continue our celebration of this renewal of our covenant with the risen Lord by eating the sacred food of his body, which makes us members of his risen body, and by drinking the blood of the new covenant, through which all the remaining days of our lives become a Passover to the glory of his resurrection.

As we begin a new academic year and a new liturgical year, may this same risen Lord enfold all our coming days into the glorious *Today* of the everlasting kingdom of the Father, the Son, and the Holy Spirit. Amen.

CHRIST, OUR BEGINNING

2 Corinthians 4:6–15; Matthew 22:35–46

Brothers and sisters who are dearly beloved in Christ Jesus our Lord:

As we begin a new academic year, we are also beginning a new liturgical year in the Byzantine tradition, in which the church year begins on September 1.

But, in our present circumstances, it is fair to ask: Do we really want to speak of a new beginning of anything, whether it be the academic year or the church year or anything else? Our present time does not seem like a time suitable for new beginnings. It does not seem to leave room for the fresh excitement and hopeful expectation that we associate with new beginnings.

We had hoped that this pandemic, with all the fear and anguish it has already caused, would be finished by now and then we would have been able to embark on a truly

---

This sermon was preached at a liturgy on September 4, 2021. Therefore, the readings are not those for the beginning of the Byzantine liturgical year on September 1. Nevertheless, I found it helpful to tie the readings to the theme of a new liturgical year and a new academic year.

new beginning. But it's not finished. Though *we* might feel relatively safe, the pandemic still rages, destroying lives and families and wreaking havoc in our society. We are still in the middle of it and unable to make a new beginning that is free from its burden.

But even before and apart from this pandemic, it seems that our poor human race and this poor world are just too old and tired and corrupted to make for new beginnings. When we think of the now daily catastrophes of climate change and the scientifically calculated doom that awaits our whole planet in the terrifyingly foreseeable future, it seems far more realistic to think of endings rather than beginnings. And then there are all the old evils that never leave us: injustice, hatred, godlessness, greed, natural disasters of all sorts.

All these go on and on, without end. Where, in all this, is there really time and space for a new beginning? What does it mean, in the midst of all this oldness of the world, to celebrate a new beginning of anything—whether it be the school year or the church year or anything else?

My brothers and sisters, the truth is that this world, considered in itself, has always been old. It never had staying power. Ever since sin entered the world, this world has been old, sick, and senile, racing toward its own destruction. Long before anybody heard of climate change or nuclear and chemical and biological warfare, the prophet Isaiah said,

> Lift up your eyes to the heavens,
> and look at the earth beneath;
> for the heavens will vanish like smoke,

Isa. 51:6
> the earth will wear out like a garment,
> and those who live on it will die like gnats,
> but my salvation will be forever,
> and my deliverance will never be ended.

The earth will wear out like a garment: It seems that we can see that now even with our physical eyes and we can measure the wearing out of the world with scientific instruments.

But my salvation will be forever, and my deliverance will never be ended: Here, then, my brothers and sisters, is our new beginning. Only the God who, in the beginning, created this world from nothing can heal it from the oldness and corruption of sin and restore its original newness and grant it a new beginning.

But we have heard and we believe—and therefore we speak—the good news that God has already brought about this new beginning, this salvation and deliverance that will be forever and will never be ended, through our Lord Jesus Christ. He is the Word, who was in the beginning, through whom all things have their beginning. He is the eternal radiance of the Father's light who became the light of the world when the Father said, at the very beginning of creation, "Let light shine out of darkness. Let there be light." And when this world became darkened again and old through sin, he took flesh and clothed himself with the worn-out garment of this world and washed it in his blood and he sent the Holy Spirit to shine in our hearts "the light of the knowledge of the glory of God in the face of Jesus Christ."

2 Cor. 4:13

John 1:1–2

John 1:3–4
Heb. 1:3
Gen. 1:3

2 Cor. 4:6

So, *yes*, we *can* celebrate the beginning—not just of the school year or even the church year. We can and must make use of every time and every occasion and every day to celebrate the Eternal Beginning who has entered our world and made it forever new, our Lord Jesus Christ. In him, we always have a new beginning, a new beginning that never ends and never gets old. It doesn't matter how old the world gets. This world has always been old, but our God is forever new.

As long as we are in this world, we must suffer the oldness of the world. But as much as we are in Christ, we are always celebrating a new and never-ending beginning. As long as we are living in this world, we do not have the option of not getting old and not suffering the oldness of the world. And it is not God's will that we be utterly untouched by the oldness of the world. Just as our Lord himself entered our old world and allowed himself to be killed by it in order to put to death its oldness and renew it in himself, so we too carry the treasure of the newness of Christ in *2 Cor. 4:7*   earthen jars, jars made of the old and corrupted earth.

And so we must submit to being afflicted and perplexed and struck down by this old and fallen world, *2 Cor. 4:10*   and in this way "we carry in our body the death of Jesus," which puts to death the oldness of this world. Because we are in Christ, we not only die with the world but in that very dying with the world, we die to the world and put *Col. 3:5*   to death everything in us that is merely of this world.

But, through the power that raised Jesus from the dead, our dying with the world and our dying to the world is our birth into the indestructible newness that Christ brought into the world through his resurrection. Since we already live by the new power of this resurrection, we are not crushed in our afflictions; we do not despair in our perplexity; we are not forsaken when we are persecuted; *2 Cor. 4:8–10*   we are not destroyed when we are struck down. And in this way, the new life of the risen Lord becomes visible in *2 Cor. 4:10*   our mortal flesh to all the world.

And so, my brothers and sisters, every day in Christ we get newer and newer. The world around us may show every sign of hastening to its end. But even as we suffer with everyone else the death pangs of this passing world, for us they *Matt. 24:8*   are transformed into the birth pangs of the new creation, *Rom. 8:22*   of which we are the firstfruits and ambassadors. While the *1 Cor. 15:20*   world rushes to its inevitable end, we are every day coming *2 Cor. 5:20*   closer to the beginning. In Christ and by the power of his Spirit, we learn to exist more and more *in the beginning*.

If we ask what it means to exist "in the beginning," we hear a clear and simple and powerful answer to that question in our Lord's words in today's gospel. To exist in the beginning is to exist in love. Love is the beginning because God is the Beginning and "God is Love." It was in love and out of love that God created the world in the beginning. The commandment to love God with all our heart and all our strength and all our mind is a commandment to exist in the beginning, to exist in the radiance of the light that is the beginning, the eternal beginning that is always new and never gets old.

1 John 4:8

Heb. 1:3
John 1:4

As long as we keep this commandment of love, it is a new commandment because it guards us in the newness of the life of God. But when we allow ourselves to be enslaved to sin, it becomes merely an old commandment, a commandment that has lost its luster, a commandment that is merely repeated rather than enacted, a commandment that becomes burdensome and even impossible. Yet, when we turn again to our Lord Jesus Christ, in whom Love itself became flesh, he makes it again a new commandment for us by making us capable of the ever-new life of loving God and loving each other through him and in the power of his Spirit. As the apostle John says, "God's love was revealed among us in this way: God sent his only Son into the world so that we might live through him." And we can add: "so that we might *love* through him."

1 John 2:8

1 John 4:9

So, my brothers and sisters, let us indeed celebrate the beginning. By all means, let us make use of the beginning of the academic year and the beginning of the church year to celebrate the beginning of all things, the Eternal Beginning who has come into this world to renew it with a new beginning that will never end.

We do not need to delude ourselves by thinking that this world, in itself, has any power to renew itself or to generate a new beginning for itself. The form of this world

1 Cor. 7:31   is passing away and it is passing away before our very eyes. But our faith assures us that it is not passing away into oblivion but is rather passing over to the new heaven and

Rev. 21:1   new earth that have already entered this world through our Lord Jesus Christ. So, let us die to this old world even as we are dying with it; let us live, through love, in the new world that has already been established in Christ.

And let us now celebrate the never-ending beginning of the new life we have in Christ by eating and drinking his love that renews all things. Let us eat the body of his love and drink the blood of his love—the love of God our Father that we receive through the abundant grace of our Lord Jesus Christ and the communion of the Holy Spirit. Amen.

EXALTATION OF THE HOLY CROSS

THE LURE OF THE CROSS

Galatians 2:16–21; Mark 8:34–9:1

Brothers and sisters, who are dearly beloved in Jesus Christ, our Lord:

The last time we gathered in this chapel, on the first day of the Byzantine liturgical year, we heard the Lord Jesus announce his mission to proclaim good news to the poor, liberty to the captives, and to announce the year of the Lord's favor. And we recognized that Jesus continues this mission at every Divine Liturgy. Every liturgical year is the year of the Lord's favor, the Lord's grace, in which the living God bestows upon us grace upon grace, transforming our lives into the likeness of his divine life, even as the wine and bread we offer are transformed into his body and blood.

Today, as we celebrate the Exaltation of the Holy Cross, the Lord Jesus announces to us the good news that

---

This sermon and the next were both preached on Sundays following the Feast of the Exaltation of the Holy Cross on September 14. They focus on the theme of that feast but the Scripture readings differ from those prescribed for the feast day itself, which are the following: 1 Corinthians 1:18–24; John 19:6–11, 13–20, 25–28, 30–35.

our communion with him and the transformation of our
lives into the likeness of his divine life, can only happen if
we carry our cross and follow him—if we have communion with his cross, and can say with St. Paul, "I am crucified with him. It is now no longer I who live, but Christ
Gal. 2:20   is living in me. And the life I now live in the flesh, I live
within the faith in the Son of God who loved me and gave
himself up for me."

The historical event behind the Feast of the Exaltation
of the Holy Cross is the finding of the cross on which
Jesus was crucified by the empress Helena, the mother
of the emperor Constantine, in the fourth century. Before that time, the cross of Christ and his tomb had been
covered over by a pagan temple that was built by another
Roman emperor, Hadrian. The story goes that the emperor Constantine had a vision of the cross, along with a
banner that said, "By this sign you shall conquer," and so
he sent out his mother to find the cross on which Jesus
was crucified.

Now, I think it's okay to be suspicious of Constantine's
motives and his whole understanding of the meaning of
the cross, beginning with his seeming to interpret today's
gospel as if Jesus said, "Whoever wishes to follow me,
let him get his mom to take up the cross and come after
me." Maybe a lot of us secretly and subconsciously hold
this interpretation, but I don't want to get too much into
psychotherapy here!

But today, we are not celebrating the feast of the exaltation of Constantine or the exaltation of Helena, but the
exaltation of the *cross*. What is the exaltation of the cross,
then, that we are celebrating today?

What we are celebrating today is the *lure* of the cross,
the strangely seductive power of the cross, the power of

the cross to tug at our hearts and pull us toward it by an irresistible force of grace, often against what seems to be our better judgment by worldly standards. It is this power of attraction of the cross by which it galvanizes our hearts and draws them toward it, which Jesus referred to when he said, "When I am lifted up, I will draw all people to myself." As if to say: "When I am lifted up on the cross, my cross will draw the hearts of all people to the heart of my crucified love."

John 12:32

This is the lure of the cross that makes even kings and emperors feel that they are *lacking* something, that they are inadequate and impoverished if they don't associate themselves *somehow* with the cross.

My brothers and sisters, we can make fun of Constantine and Helena and we can be suspicious and critical of the association of the cross and imperial power. But attending to God's artful providence, and his power to transform human foolishness into his own wisdom, we can find a deep and significant meaning in the fact that we celebrate today the finding of the cross by the empress Helena. What edifying and salvific meaning can we find in the seemingly awkward association that we find in this liturgical feast between the cross and imperial power?

1 Cor. 1:25

I believe that at least part of this meaning is that the message of the cross is addressed, in the first place, to our *imperial* selves. Whatever we do, whether we are professors or students or something else, deep-down, we all see ourselves as emperors and empresses, as Constantine or Helena. We seek power and prestige and we prefer to be served rather than to serve.

But today, while we are still in the opening weeks of the liturgical year, the church confronts our imperial selves with the lure of the cross. Today, the church invites us to look upon the sacrificial love of Jesus, his inexhaustible and indestructible and completely defenseless love displayed on the cross. And when we look upon this love displayed on the cross, we feel the poverty and sadness and petty inadequacy of our imperial selves. And, by the grace of God, we go in search of the cross. To go in search of the cross does not mean that we go in search of pain and suffering for its own sake. But we go in search of this inexhaustible and indestructible and completely defenseless love of Jesus that led him to the cross.

In today's epistle, St. Paul tells us that no one is justified by the works of the law but only by faith in Jesus Christ. This too applies to the lure of the cross and our communion in the cross of Christ. A lot can go wrong if we think of carrying the cross as a human work, something we do in response to a divine commandment imposed upon us. It is this way of thinking that leads to a morbid exaltation of suffering for its own sake and that also makes us secretly resentful that God has burdened us with all kinds of suffering and commands us to bear this suffering in order to earn salvation.

Gal. 2:16

No, the true cross is a *gift*; it's a grace. It's the self-giving love of Jesus that is granted to us through the Holy Spirit poured out into our hearts. The sign that we have received this gift is that we feel a joyful urge to leave everything and follow Christ, to follow him wherever he goes, even to death on the cross.

Rom. 5:5

On the other hand, the sign that we are not ready to receive this gift is that we feel a certain sadness that comes with the recognition that we are not willing to give up everything to follow Christ—because we are afraid of the cost. The gospel tells us about this sadness when it speaks of Jesus's invitation to the rich young man to sell all his possessions and follow him. The gospel tells us: "When the young man heard this, he went away sad because he had many possessions." He went away sad because he was imprisoned in the poverty of his imperial self and could not accept the liberation that Jesus offered, which is the freedom of God's reckless and limitless love that led Jesus to the cross. *Mark 10:22*

My brothers and sisters, today the risen Lord comes to us in this liturgy to proclaim this freedom and this liberation from the captivity of our imperial selves. When he tells us to take up our cross and follow him, he is not making us captive to yet another commandment of the law, harsher than all the rest. By this commandment, he is in fact granting us the Lord's favor, the Lord's grace in the form of the freedom of the cross, the liberation of perfect sacrificial love.

Each of us will have to discern in prayer how we should go in search of the grace of the cross in our lives and how we can persevere and even rejoice in that grace, by the power of the Spirit. But we are now invited in this liturgy to receive this grace, this liberation, this power of Christ's inexhaustible, indestructible, and completely defenseless love—which is offered to us through communion with the body and blood, the life and death, of our Lord Jesus Christ. It is only by eating his body that was broken for us that we receive the power to break ourselves open through the sacrificial love of the cross. It is only by drinking his blood that was poured out for us that we receive the power to pour ourselves out in self-giving love. And then we will be able to hear Jesus say to us, in the Spirit: "Amen I say to you, there are some of those standing here who will not taste death, till they have seen the kingdom of God coming in power." *Mark 9:1*

Let us now eat and drink from the spiritual nourishment that gives us the grace to carry the cross and that illumines our minds to see hidden in the cross the coming in power of the kingdom of God, the kingdom of the only true and glorious God who is all-powerful in his love and defenseless in his mercy, the Father, the Son, and the Holy Spirit. Amen.

The Cross and
the Happiness of God

Galatians 2:16–21; Mark 8:34–9:1

Brothers and sisters who are dearly beloved in Jesus Christ
our Lord:

Today, we continue our celebration of the Exaltation
of the Holy Cross. There are three times in the liturgical
year at which the Byzantine liturgy draws us into the mystery of the cross of our Lord, and each of these focuses on
a different aspect of the mystery.

On the third Sunday of Lent, we celebrate the mystery
of the Holy Cross as we prepare to reinitiate ourselves into
the mystery of the Lord's passion and resurrection.

On Holy Friday, we contemplate the divine self-
emptying of our Lord, who allowed himself to be humanly killed by his own creation. We sing: "He who hung
the earth upon the waters is hung upon the tree."

The Feast of the Exaltation of the Holy Cross, which
we are now celebrating, is distinctive in its emphasis on
the brightness of the cross—the cross as a source of joy,
of triumph, of exaltation.

Underlying all the extravagant and poetic language in which the liturgy speaks about the glory of the cross on this feast, there is one simple and startling claim: that the way of the cross is the only way of genuine happiness. The claim is not that the way of the cross is the only way *to* genuine happiness, as if following the cross *now* leads to happiness *later*, after we die and are resurrected. That is not the claim. The claim is that the way of the cross is the only way of genuine happiness, here and now. There is no other way to be genuinely happy *on this earth* except by carrying the cross.

Of course, this claim is shocking for us because it flies directly against our natural inclination to think that happiness consists in maximizing our pleasure and minimizing our pain. How, then, can the cross, which we associate with pain and suffering, be the only genuine way of happiness?

But, my brothers and sisters, to think of happiness as merely the maximization of pleasure and the minimization of pain is to think only in a human way, according to the flesh, and not to think in a divine way, according to the Spirit. It was in this fleshly way that the apostle Peter was thinking when he tried to dissuade our Lord from the way of the cross. And we know how our Lord replied to him: "Get behind me, Satan; for you are setting your mind not on divine things but on human things."

Mark 8:33

Now, if we want to set our mind on divine things and not on human things, we have to think of happiness in a divine way and not in a merely human way. And in order to do that, we should start by asking this question: How did God himself find happiness while he was in human form on this earth? How did the only begotten Son of God, who is God from God and Light from Light, try to live out his divine happiness when he became incarnate in human flesh?

It would be a great mistake to think that our Lord Jesus Christ did not seek happiness while he was on earth. Every rational human being, who is mentally and emotionally healthy, seeks happiness. And our Lord Jesus Christ, being Divine Reason itself, the Logos, was in his humanity a supremely rational human being who was mentally and emotionally healthy in the most perfect way.

Moreover, the teaching of the church on the mystery of the incarnation instructs us that our Lord always conformed his humanity to his divinity. While the human being was originally created in the image and likeness of God, it is only in Jesus Christ that humanity achieved the perfection of its imaging of God and its likeness to God. We must believe, therefore, that in his human search for happiness, Jesus was perfectly imaging the perfect happiness of God. In his divinity, our Lord Jesus was filled with the perfect happiness of God. In his humanity, he always aspired to live out the divine happiness according to the mode of human nature.

Now, what was the path that the Lord chose in order to humanly live the happiness of God? It was the path of the cross. As shocking as that may be if we set our mind on human things and not on divine things, it makes perfect sense once we consider the divine things revealed to us through the humanity of our Lord Jesus Christ.

Our Lord taught us, by word and deed, that the divine happiness consists in the perfect glory and perfect blessedness of God's perfectly generous and self-giving love. Of course, Jesus could not have lived out in his humanity the perfect glory of God's perfectly generous and self-giving love just by maximizing his own pleasure and minimizing his own pain. There is no perfect glory of God's self-giving love in that. Even the lowest beasts instinctually seek to maximize their pleasure and minimize their pain. God's happiness is very different from that. God's perfect happiness consists in God's perfect joy in his perfect love.

Once we have set our minds on divine things and not on human things and consider what happiness really is from the point of view of God's own happiness, we can see clearly that the only way that Jesus could have lived out in his humanity the perfect happiness of God's perfect love was the way that he did choose: the way of the cross, the way of opening his heart wide enough to enfold all the suffering in the world and fill it with his perfectly generous and self-giving love.

And so, not just at the end of his life, but throughout his life, Jesus always sought his happiness on earth not by maximizing his own pleasure and minimizing his own pain but by seeking out all those who suffer and offering them the healing and saving love of the Father. That was the happiness that Jesus aspired to throughout his human life. It was the happiness of the cross. Yes, it was a crucified happiness but still a genuine happiness and a true fulfillment, if we think of happiness and fulfillment in a divine way and not in a merely human way.

My brothers and sisters, this is the happiness that our Lord offers us today, at this liturgy, as we continue our celebration of the Exaltation of the Cross. He says to each of us today, "If you wish to share in my human imaging and likeness of God's happiness, you must forsake the way of seeking only to maximize pleasure and minimize pain. You must seek to embrace the suffering of this sinful world through my perfect love."

My brothers and sisters, of course we cannot walk on this path of the crucified happiness of God's perfect love by our own strength and our own power. It is after all a divine happiness we are seeking in the poor earthen vessels of our flesh. We can only walk on this path if we can say with St. Paul:

"It is no longer I who live, but it is Christ who   *Gal. 2:20–21*
    lives in me.
And the life I now live in the flesh—
the life I now live in the flesh that seeks only
    to maximize its pleasure and minimize
    its pain—
I live this life in the flesh by faith in the Son
    of God,
who loved me and gave himself for me.
I now live by faith that the only genuine happi-
    ness is the happiness of God's perfect love,
God's perfectly generous and self-emptying love.
Even if, in this world of sin, this divine
    happiness must be lived out as a crucified
    happiness,
it is still the only true and genuine happiness
    to be found on this earth,
the only happiness on earth that is the image
    and likeness of God's own perfect happi-
    ness in eternity,
which we will know perfectly in heaven if
    we have lived it, however imperfectly,
    on earth."

My brothers and sisters, if we are able to say all this by the power of the Spirit of Christ in us, then we will have attained the gift of being able to carry our cross through the grace of our Lord Jesus Christ. And then we will not taste death until we see the kingdom of God come with power. Because the very act of carrying the cross is itself the manifestation of the kingdom of God coming with power. When we carry the cross, we already enter the kingdom of God's power. When we carry the cross, we already have a share in the power of God's happiness, which is the power of God's joy in his own love. And this power of God's perfect joy in his own love, which has overcome all suffering through the resurrection of our Lord, will empower us to bear our sufferings and the suffering of the whole world, in love.

Let us now prepare ourselves to taste and eat and drink the life of the One who tasted death on behalf of all, so that we might no longer fear death and suffering and might become free to live out God's perfect love without count- *Heb. 2:9, 15*   ing the cost. Let us now taste the fruit of that love which conquered death and gave us a share in God's perfect love, through which we have become crucified to the world in order to save the world and fill it with God's perfect love. May we be filled with this love that is given to us through our sharing in the body and blood of our crucified and exalted Lord Jesus Christ, by the power of the Spirit of his love, to the glory of God the Father. Amen.

Boasting in the Cross
of Christ

Galatians 2:16–21; Mark 8:34–9:1

Brothers and sisters who are dearly beloved in Christ Jesus our Lord:

Today is the first Sunday after the Exaltation of the Holy Cross and we continue our celebration of that feast.

As many of you know, in this feast we celebrate the finding of the physical cross upon which our Lord was crucified, by Helena, the mother of the emperor Constantine, in the fourth century. But, more significantly, this feast invites each of us to find exaltation in our experience of the cross in our own lives. This feast invites us, and offers us the grace, to make the exaltation of the cross the foundation of our lives.

But what does it mean to make the exaltation of the cross the foundation of our lives? I think that the key to answering that question is something that St. Paul says near the end of his epistle to the Galatians. He says: "May I never boast of anything except the cross of our Lord Jesus Christ, by which the world has been crucified

Gal. 6:14 to me, and I to the world." If we can say with St. Paul that we never want to boast of anything except the cross, we would definitely be well on our way to making the exaltation of the cross the foundation of our lives. But, then, it does seem very odd to associate the cross with boasting. What does it mean to boast in the cross?

Well, let's think about boasting for a minute. All of us, to some degree, are prone to boasting. Some of us are good at boasting, some of us are not so good. Some of us are obvious and artless and relentless in our boasting; some of us are more subtle and more understated and sophisticated in our boasting. But we're all at least inclined to boast. To a great measure, being successful in our society requires knowing how to boast well—how to boast in just the right way, at just the right times, in just the right measure. As we embark on another academic year, we are all trying to do things that we can boast about, and boasting itself will be one of our recurring tasks.

Now, let's also think about why it is that people who are obvious and constant boasters are annoying and hard to be with. I think there are two answers to that question. First, somebody who is always boasting about himself doesn't give me a chance to boast about myself! But secondly, and more importantly, someone who is always boasting can seem literally unlovable. Not just because somebody like that turns people off, but even more, because the person who is always boasting just doesn't give you a chance to actually love them. They don't seem open to being just loved. Instead, they are always trying to coerce admiration and respect and attention on the basis of their achievements, their works. In this way, they don't seem open to just receiving our love as a gift.

Of course, the tragic thing about that is that the deepest root of our desire to boast is the desire to be loved.

Though we're always trying to boast on the basis of our works, isn't it true that the only thing worth boasting about, the only thing worth exulting in, is simply being loved? What does it matter if I have all kinds of accomplishments, and I've performed all kinds of works, and there is no one who loves me? If I can't boast of being loved, is there any real value in all the other achievements that I boast about?

In the end, loving and being loved are really the only things worth boasting about. When our boasting comes out of the experience of being loved and of loving, this boasting is good and wholesome and full of a wholesome exultation. I remember when one of my children started kindergarten and the parents were invited to a little concert in which the children were singing. And just before they were about to start singing, my son jumped out of line and yelled out, "Look at me, Dad. Look at me. I'm right here. Look at me!" Now, the wonderful thing about that incident for me is that he was boasting before the concert even began, before anyone actually did anything. He was boasting—was presenting himself for admiration—not on the basis of any achievement, but simply out of the confidence and the exultation of being loved. This was a boasting not on the basis of works, but on the basis of love.

For St. Paul, boasting in the cross is also first and foremost a boasting about love, about God's love for us manifested on the cross. It is crucial for him that we do not ruin that boasting by claiming to have earned God's love through our works. Boasting of our accomplishments before God makes us unlovable before God—not because God is turned off by our boasting but because that kind of boasting in our own works does not allow us to receive the free gift of God's love in Christ. Not only that, but when we

boast of our own works before God—as the Pharisee does
Luke 18:9–14   in the parable—we do not allow God to boast of his love for
us, the love that led him to the cross for our salvation.

Our boasting in the cross, then, is above all, our boasting in God's love for us. We boast for the very good reason
that we are *divinely loved*. And that is the greatest boast
imaginable—that we are loved not just by this or that human being, but by the One who is Perfect Being in himself, who so loved the world that he sent his only begotten
John 3:16   Son to love us even to the point of death on the cross.
Phil. 2:8   While we were still enemies of God, and had nothing to
Rom. 5:10   boast about before God, when our lack of righteousness
should have been a source of shame and rejection before
the all-holy righteousness of God, God wanted to boast
of the extent of his love for us by taking away our shame
and becoming our righteousness through his death on
2 Cor. 5:21   the cross. So, when we boast in the cross we are letting
God boast of his love for us and we are boasting about
this love.

At the same time, it is precisely our boasting in the
cross that brings about our being crucified to the world
and the world being crucified to us. That is because, as
soon as we begin to experience the love of God that led
Jesus to the cross, we become impelled by that love to
cease living for ourselves and to live only for the One who
2 Cor. 5:15   loved us and gave himself for us.

And in this way, we learn to become ever more eager
to carry our cross and follow Christ because we want to
boast not only in being the objects of his love but also
in practicing the kind of radical self-giving love that he
showed us on the cross. And in this way, too, as St. Paul
Rom. 5:3   tells us elsewhere, we learn to boast even in our sufferings,
knowing that Christ's love accompanies us in our suffer-
ing and transfigures our suffering through the Holy Spirit
that he continually pours out into our hearts.

As we learn to grow in our boasting in the cross, no matter what sufferings and humiliations we may have to endure, we will find ourselves impelled again and again to step out of the chorus of the world's boasting, and yell out, with all the power of God's own Spirit, "Look at me, Father, look at me, I'm right here, in your Son, look at me! Look at the one you love; look at me learning to love like you." Indeed, he is looking down upon all of us as we celebrate this liturgy and he is rejoicing in our desire to be granted the grace of boasting in his love for us, which he demonstrated on the cross.

My brothers and sisters, in the world, it is a good occasion for boasting if we are invited to a fancy dinner, hosted by an important person, in which we are served expensive food and rare wine. How much greater must be our boasting, then, as we now sing with the angels before the heavenly throne and prepare to partake of the precious body and holy blood of the King of kings and Lord of lords, our Savior Jesus Christ! As we partake of this meal of God's sacrificial love for us, may the Holy Spirit fill us with ever-greater boasting as we grow in the knowledge of the breadth and length and height and depth of the love of Christ manifested for us on the cross, to the eternal glory *Eph. 3:18* of God our Father. Amen.

THE THEOTOKOS ENTERS THE TEMPLE

Mary's Self-Dedication
to the Lord

Hebrews 9:1–7; Luke 10:38–42; 11:27–28

Brothers and sisters who are dearly beloved in Christ Jesus our Lord:

Today, we celebrate the Feast of the Entrance of the Mother of God into the Temple. According to tradition—as testified in the second-century Book of James or *Protevangelium*—Mary was dedicated to the Lord, as a three-year-old child, by her parents, Joachim and Anne. At this ceremony of dedication, the high priest Zacharias took the child Mary into the holy of holies, where customarily the priest is only allowed to enter once a year, on Yom Kippur, the Day of Atonement. The grace of God descended on Mary and she began to dance in the temple and lived there until she was betrothed to Joseph.

Now, it is possible to respond to this story by saying that none of this can be found in the canonical Scriptures nor is it the dogmatic teaching of any church council and so one can take it as just a pious legend and leave it at that.

And yet, it is a liturgical feast, and that fact obligates us to believe that there is a real grace offered to us at this liturgy, a saving and sanctifying grace that goes far beyond merely affirming or denying the historicity of this story. The grace that is offered to us at today's liturgy is that of preparing ourselves to receive a renewal of Christ's presence and power in us. Mary, the Mother of God, is sacramentally present with us today at this liturgy, and presents herself to us as a model for that preparation.

The theological truth that this feast is conveying to us is elsewhere expressed by the common motif among the church fathers that Jesus did not pass through Mary "as through a tube" but really took his flesh from her.* On the one hand, this statement is about what Jesus *received* from Mary. It wants to affirm the true humanity of Jesus as derived from Mary's flesh and blood. Jesus didn't just come with his own self-made flesh, as it were, and just pass through Mary's body, but he genuinely received his flesh from Mary's flesh. On the other hand, it is also a statement about what Mary *gave* to Jesus. Mary gave her flesh to Jesus, just like any mother gives her own flesh to her child.

What this particular feast wants to emphasize is that Mary's preparation to give her flesh to Jesus took over her whole life. Before conceiving Jesus, Mary spent her whole life preparing to conceive him. By God's grace, she was guided throughout her life to prepare herself for that moment when the Holy Spirit came upon her and the power of the Most High overshadowed her and she conceived the Son of the Most High.

We often see that mothers are led by a kind of instinct, which is as much emotional and spiritual as it is physical, to make special preparations for conceiving and carrying a child. Often, an expecting mother will give up drinking

---

* See, for example, Irenaeus, *Against Heresies* 3.11.3.

alcohol or smoking and will try to eat healthy food and to exercise in order to make her body as hospitable as possible for the new child. Sometimes, even those who are addicted to drugs are motivated to cleanse and purify themselves in preparation for carrying a child, and if they don't do this, we consider it an aberration. If the expectant mother is spiritually mature, she will also want to spend some extra time in prayer and will almost effortlessly slip into a more contemplative frame of mind as she is over-taken by the awesome mystery of collaborating with God in the work of creating a new human being.

Both this feast and other church teachings about the purity of Mary's body and soul are basically telling us that all this preparation of body and spirit—which all mothers are motivated to do by a kind of instinct—took place in Mary to a superlative degree and with the maximal cooperation of divine grace. In preparing for his only begotten Son to dwell in human flesh, God allowed our human nature to undergo a kind of detoxification in Mary's body and soul.

But Mary did not just accept this grace passively. She embraced it freely and collaborated with it at every moment of her life. The message of today's feast of the Presentation of Mary at the Temple is that Mary's col-laboration with this grace was the work of her whole life. She was presented at the temple as a child and she lived in the temple until she herself became the new and more perfect temple in which the living God took flesh. And so we sing at the Orthros service for this feast: "Today the living Temple of the Great King enters the Temple to be prepared as a divine dwelling place for Him. O people, rejoice exceedingly!"*

* Mattins for Feast of Entrance of Theotokos into the Temple. *The Festal Menaion*, trans. Mother Mary and Archimandrite Kallistos Ware (South Canaan, PA: St. Tikhon's Seminary Press, 1998), 174 (altered).

My brothers and sisters, it is not without significance that we celebrate this feast of Mary's Entrance into the Temple as we are preparing for the feast of the Nativity of our Lord—the Feast of Christmas. Every Christmas, we are offered the grace of a new birth of the presence and power of Christ in us. Every Christmas, we become sharers in Mary's grace of being the Mother of God. Every Christmas, we are called to become anew a living temple of God, a divine dwelling place for Christ, just as Mary was and is.

But for all that to happen as it should, we need to prepare for it. Like any mother who is expecting to give birth, we need to purify our bodies and souls in order to prepare ourselves to give a new birth to Christ in us. We need to enter into the holy of holies, into the inner sanctuary of deep and fervent prayer, in order to receive Christ, who wishes to be born anew in us.

We do not expect a mother who is about to give birth to be getting drunk at parties in the last weeks of her pregnancy. Neither should we spend the weeks before Christmas in frivolity and secular distraction, but as the apostle said, "Let us live honorably as in the day, not in revelry and drunkenness, not in debauchery and licentiousness, *Rom. 13:13–14*   not in quarreling and jealousy. Instead, put on the Lord Jesus Christ, and make no provisions for the desires of the flesh."

So, my brothers and sisters, today the Mother of God calls us to enter with her into the temple of preparation for the coming of Christ, so that each one of us can become a temple and a dwelling place for Christ. As Mary was presented to the temple and entered into the holy of holies, let us now present ourselves at the altar and eat the body and drink the blood of our most High and Holy God, Jesus Christ. May our souls and bodies grow in communion with him until we celebrate the great feast of his Nativity, in which he will be newly manifested to the world through his new birth in us, through the intercession of his most pure Mother, who joins us now as we give glory and praise to the one and only true God, the Father, the Son, and the Holy Spirit. Amen.

CHRISTMAS SEASON

A Crippled Humanity
Awaits Its Salvation

Galatians 5:22–6:2; Luke 13:10–17

My brothers and sisters who are dearly beloved in Christ Jesus our Lord:

Most of us are familiar with the Christmas hymn "God Rest Ye Merry Gentlemen," which sings of the "tidings of comfort and joy" of the Christmas season. But in this Advent season, as we prepare ourselves to celebrate these tidings of comfort and joy, it is important to recognize that Christmas is not the celebration of the comfort and joy that are *already present* in our lives, or that are already there in the world if only we look on the bright side of things. Rather, we look forward to Christmas for the grace of new comfort in the midst of our old afflictions and new joy in the midst of our old sorrows.

After all, if we go back to that hymn, "God Rest Ye Merry Gentlemen," it tells us that our comfort and joy is to "remember Christ our Savior / was born on Christmas day / to save us all from Satan's power / when we were gone astray."

It is only in this light that we can see how our gospel reading for today fits in with our Advent preparations for

Christmas. Today's gospel tells us about a woman who was saved from Satan's power by Christ our Savior. This woman was crippled and permanently bent down, unable to stand upright. Satan had bound her for eighteen years and the Lord Jesus set her free from her bondage, despite the protestations of the leader of the synagogue.

Perhaps some of us know someone who is physically bent over and unable to stand upright. But, in reality, it is our whole human race that is bent over, stooped down, bound by the power of Satan, and unable to stand upright. The empirical and physical evidence of the crippled condition of our whole human race is all around us: the imminent destruction of the whole planet because of our heedless consumption; our collective inability to act in unison in order to eradicate a deadly pandemic; the steadfastness of injustice; the glorification of cruelty and hatred; the rampant disdain for God and contempt for godliness. So much so that it seems that the prophet Isaiah was directly speaking of our times when he said, "The earth lies polluted under its inhabitants; for they have transgressed laws, violated the statutes, broken the everlasting covenant. Therefore, a curse devours the earth, and its inhabitants suffer for their guilt. . . . The earth is utterly broken, the earth is torn asunder. . . . The earth staggers like a drunkard, it sways like a hut; its transgression lies heavy upon it."

Isa. 24:5–6, 19–20

It is also true of each one of us that our transgression lies heavy upon us and so we are bent down and stooped over because of our sins. Each one of us can truthfully say, with the psalmist, "My iniquities have gone over my head; they weigh like a burden too heavy for me. . . . I am utterly bowed down and prostrate; all day long I go around mourning."

Ps. 38:4, 6

In this time of Advent, taking our cue from today's gospel, we should recognize all the ways in which our human race and our world is crippled and bent down with sin and suffering. And yet, this does not hinder us but impels us to look forward even more to the Christmas tidings of comfort and joy.

The comfort and joy that we are looking forward to is the wonderful good news that while we were still enemies of God, bent down and stooped over by the weight of our sins, our loving God "bent the heavens and stooped down" to enter our humanity. He stooped down to the *Ps. 18:9* degradation of our sinful humanity in order to free us from the bondage and power of Satan and to make us stand upright again, and to raise us up with him and to make us sit with him in the heavenly places, and to fill us *Eph. 2:6* with the fruits of his Spirit. In this time of Advent, we look forward to the birth in the flesh of all these fruits of the Spirit that we heard about in today's epistle. For it is Jesus himself who is Love Incarnate, who is the embodiment of joy, peace, patience, kindness, generosity, faithfulness, gentleness, and self-control, even to the point of emptying himself unto death on the cross for our salvation.

This Jesus, this embodiment of divine love and joy and peace and all the other fruits of the Spirit, has already been born; he has already stooped down from heaven and entered into our suffering and crippled world. But the world has still not acknowledged his birth in its midst. He came to his own and his own did not receive him. Like parents *John 1:11* who abandon their newborn child, our world has rejected the birth of God among us.

But to us who have received him and who believe in him, he has given the power to enter into the mystery of his birth in the flesh, to be reborn in him, to be reborn not of blood or of the will of the flesh or of the will of man, but of God. This power grows within us throughout our Chris- *John 1:13* tian journey. For a Christian, every day, every situation, every moment is an opportunity to be reborn in Christ. But it is especially during this time of Advent, in preparation for Christmas, that we are offered the grace to enter more fully into the birth of Christ and to be reborn in him.

We can only do this, however, if we recognize our crippled condition and present the burden of our sins and sufferings to Christ. In the Divine Liturgy, at the end of the Little Entrance, the priest says, "Come, let us worship and bow down before Christ."* When we bow down before Christ, we are like that crippled woman in today's gospel, who brings before Christ the burden of her bondage to the forces of evil and destruction. But, in the very act of bowing down before Christ, we are released from that bondage and raised up with Christ at the right hand of the Father.

So, my brothers and sisters, as we approach the holy table, let us truly "worship and bow down before Christ." In doing so, let us bring before Christ not only the burdens of our individual sins and sufferings but those of all our suffering and sinful world, mindful of the apostle's words: "Bear one another's burdens and so fulfill the law *Gal. 6:2* of Christ." We know that, in the holy Eucharist, our Lord himself stoops down to serve us the spiritual nourishment of his own body and blood. May this divine nourishment prepare our souls and bodies for the grace of being reborn in Christ this Christmas and receiving the fruits of his Spirit as our most treasured Christmas gifts, to the glory of God our Father. Amen.

---

* The "Little Entrance" is a procession with the gospel book during the Byzantine liturgy. The priest and people bow down just before the priest reenters the sanctuary with the gospel.

How to Excuse Yourself from the Kingdom of God

Colossians 3:4–11; Luke 14:16–24

My brothers and sisters who are dearly beloved in Christ Jesus our Lord:

It has always been a human complaint against God that God seems far and hidden, and seems not to respond to us when we call him. The psalmist gives voice to this complaint when he says: "Why, O Lord, do you stand far off? Why do you hide yourself?" and "O my God, I cry by day and you do not answer; and by night, but find no rest." *Ps. 10:1* *Ps. 22:2*

And yet the divine Scriptures reveal to us that God has the same complaint against us. From God's point of view, it is we humans who are far from him and hide from him and do not respond when he calls. This pattern of human hiding begins immediately after the sin of Adam. We are told in the Scriptures that "the man and his wife

---

In the Byzantine tradition, there are two Sundays before Christmas that are assigned specific readings in preparation for Christmas. The first of these is the Sunday of the Holy Ancestors of Christ, for which this homily was preached.

hid themselves from the presence of the Lord. . . . But the Lord God called to the man and said 'Where are you?' and the man said, 'I heard the sound of you in the garden *Gen. 3:8–10* and I was afraid because I was naked and I hid myself.'"

Later, the prophets become the messengers of God's complaint that human beings keep hiding from him, keep rejecting him. Through the prophet Jeremiah, God says, "My people . . . have forsaken me, the fountain of living *Jer. 2:13* water, and dug out cisterns for themselves, cracked cisterns that hold no water."

In today's gospel, Jesus takes up this prophetic tradition of voicing God's complaint of being rejected by his people. He tells a parable about a man who invites people to his party and they all make excuses and reject the invitation. Imagine going through all the trouble and excitement of preparing a big party and then everybody you invite decides not to come. Jesus is telling us that this is God's position in his relation to us.

Jesus's listeners would have understood that the party that he's talking about is in fact the messianic banquet, which the prophet Isaiah described when he said, "On this mountain the Lord of Hosts will make for all people *Isa. 25* a feast of rich food, a feast of well-aged wines. . . . And he will destroy on this mountain the shroud that is cast over all people . . . and he will swallow up death forever."

But the people who were listening to Jesus could not have imagined everything that Jesus meant when he talked about God's invitation to this "great dinner"—that it meant the coming of God's kingdom on earth, the becoming human of God's only begotten Son, the sending of the Holy Spirit into our hearts, the divinization of humanity, our full and unobstructed access to the divine life of the Holy Trinity.

We know all this now and yet I'm not at all sure that we really accept Jesus's invitation either. Isn't it true that we refuse to take seriously the premise of the whole invitation, which is the announcement, "Come, for everything is ready *now*." This means: the kingdom of God is already here now. And yet, this premise is precisely what we have a very hard time accepting. Instead, we keep thinking that the dinner is actually not ready now, so we're just going to wait until we think it's really ready, after we die or after the world ends or something, as long as it is not *now*.

Luke 14:17

My brothers and sisters, this parable that we hear in today's gospel is in fact the foundation of Jesus's whole message, which is that the kingdom of God is here now. Jesus insisted from the beginning to the end of his earthly ministry that the kingdom of God has now arrived in him and we are all invited to become full citizens of this kingdom now. Jesus's message was not, "Behold, there will be a kingdom of God after you die," but "Repent, the kingdom of God is at hand, as close as your hand; it's right in front of you, it's here." This message is repeated for us in the Byzantine liturgy, when the priest says, "You have not ceased doing everything until you brought us to heaven and graciously gave us your future kingdom." "You *gave* us your future kingdom." That means that God's kingdom, which will triumph over every enemy in the future, has already been given to us who follow Christ *now*.

Why then do we not fully accept this invitation to become full citizens of the kingdom of God, right now? Maybe it seems to us that the excuses of the people in the parable in today's gospel are transparently silly and that we would not offer such silly excuses. "I bought a farm and I have to go look at it"—as if he bought the farm in the first place without looking at it!

But then what is our excuse? If we think that the excuses voiced in the parable are too lame, maybe it would be helpful for us to come up with some *real* excuses of why we don't take seriously Jesus's invitation to live fully in the kingdom of God now, an invitation that is renewed for us at every Christmas season. By "real excuses," I don't mean excuses that are justifiable, but excuses that express the real reasons why we are reluctant to accept this invitation. I can think of at least four excuses:

1. The first excuse is that, if we picture God's kingdom as a banquet or a party, then we can say that God's parties are too wild and unpredictable. Crazy things happen at God's parties. People who take seriously the message that the kingdom is here now end up doing crazy things, like giving all their possessions to the poor, or going to the desert to pray unceasingly, or just living a life that is totally dedicated to the kingdom in a way that turns the world and its values upside down. Maybe it's better not to live upside down like that, and to say to the Lord, "Please, hold me excused."

2. Another excuse is that the kingdom of God, despite being wild and unpredictable, is also strangely ordinary in a very unsettling way. In God's kingdom, we receive the life of the eternal God by eating a little bread dipped in wine; when we shake the hand of a stranger, Christ says, *Matt. 25:40* "That was really me"; when we confess our sins, we are actually destroying death and trampling on the devil. It's like a reverse special-effects thing going on. Everything we do has cosmic significance, but it's all in the form of very un-special effects. So there's both too much meaning and too little entertainment going on, so "Lord, please hold me excused."

3. Another excuse is that God's banquet tends to be full of unsavory people. One good thing about online invitations is that you can tell who else is coming and that can help you make up your mind if you want to accept the invitation. It's easy to accept an invitation in which you can see that all the people there will be beautiful people:

successful, smart, well dressed, influential, respectable, glamorous in some way or another. But God's banquet, as we can see from today's parable, gives a special place to the poor, the crippled, the lame, the blind, the suffering. These people are worthy of compassion, sure; but is hanging around them really a party? Does the kingdom of God really happen when you hang around these types of people? In that case, "Please hold me excused."

4. Finally, another excuse is that a party should be a place to relax and let off steam and release inhibitions. If we are going to talk about the kingdom of God like it's a banquet and a party and a big celebration, then you don't want advertisements for the party to say things like, "Put to death, therefore, whatever in you is earthly: impurity, evil desire, greed, anger, malice, slander. Strip off the old self with its practices." You might want to say: "Okay, I'm working on some of my faults, but if you're going to call that a party, then please hold me excused."

So, these are some of the excuses that I think we can substitute for the seemingly lame excuses we find in the gospel parable today. At least, they're more honest.

But the good news that we are celebrating today is that God has rejected all our excuses. In the Gospel of St. Luke, Jesus tells the parable that we just heard in response to someone who says to him, "Blessed is anyone who will eat bread in the kingdom of God." Brothers and sisters, *Luke 14:15* here we are, with all our excuses and all our evasions, eating bread in the kingdom of God, eating the bread of life who came down from heaven, even if we refuse to fully acknowledge and experience what it means to say that the kingdom of God is now fully present in our midst. Here we are, awaiting the celebration of the coming of God's kingdom into the world through the one who was the kingdom of God in person, our Lord Jesus Christ. In the darkness of sin and winter, we are about to celebrate again the advent of the light of God's kingdom in our midst.

At a party, sometimes it takes a while to get into the swing of things. At the beginning, things can be awkward; you make a little small talk; you have an appetizer; you can feel a little bit left out. But, then, maybe after some more food and a bit of wine and some good conversation, the party begins to have a life of its own. The kingdom of God party has now been going for a long time. It's like an all-night party. But now the night is far advanced and the day is about to dawn. It's time for us to leave behind small talk and appetizers and to partake heartily of the rich feast that God has prepared for all peoples.

Rom. 13:12

As we approach the celebration of the birth of our Lord Jesus Christ, who is the kingdom of God in person, it is time for us to embrace fully his kingdom, in all its wildness and unpredictability, in all its humility and or-dinariness, in the midst of all the suffering in the world, in the midst of our own struggles to put away the old self and clothe ourselves with the new self, which is being renewed in knowledge according to the image of its creator.

Col. 3:10

Blessed be our God, who has rejected all our rejections of him, who has excused us for all our excuses, who has compelled us by his inexhaustible grace and mercy to eat bread in his kingdom. May we eat this bread, not unto judgment or condemnation by rejecting the urgency of the announcement of God's kingdom, but by saying continually in our hearts and through our actions the opening words of this Divine Liturgy: "Blessed is the Kingdom of the Father, the Son, and the Holy Spirit, now and always and forever and ever. Amen."

The Dismal Failure
and Unimaginable Success
of the Human Race

Hebrews 11:9–10, 32–40; Matthew 1:1–25

Brothers and sisters who are dearly beloved in Christ Jesus our Lord:

On the Sunday before Christmas, our gospel reading in the Byzantine liturgy is always the genealogy of Christ, as you just heard. Often, this is an occasion for some tired humor on the part of the congregation, beginning with an exchange of rueful glances as the strange names keep piling on seemingly endlessly. It's probably also not on the top ten list of preachers' favorite texts to preach on.

But, in fact, this gospel should fill us with a deep joy and comfort and peace that makes the light of Christmas already begin to transform our hearts and minds. What this gospel tells us, in essence, is that our human race gave birth to God. Yes, we did that; we gave birth to God!

This homily was preached for the liturgy of the last Sunday before Christmas, known in the Byzantine tradition as Sunday of the Holy Genealogy.

Of course, it is true that we did not do this by our own efforts and our natural powers, and yet our efforts and our natural powers were indispensable to God's plan that, in the fullness of time, the eternal Son of God would be born in human flesh. We rightly honor and exalt Mary, the Mother of God, for bringing the human contribution to this plan to completion. But today's gospel reminds us that Mary was just the last link in a chain that goes back to the beginning of the human race and extends throughout all the doings and sufferings, all the achievements and failures of human history. *We* gave birth to God!

This is a message of consolation and affirmation that we desperately need to hear and absorb in these times of dejection and temptation to despair. If you had to grade the entire human race at this time, what grade would you give? An A+ or a D? A pass or a fail? Are we not living through a time in which the failures of our race, on so many levels, are obvious beyond denial?

But: we gave birth to God! God has chosen, in the infinite wisdom of his grace, to redeem our failures and dignify our shame and infinitely elevate all our achievements by becoming one of us, becoming like us in all Heb. 4:15   things except sin so that he can take away our sins and 2 Pet. 1:4   make us sharers in his divine life.

We can recount all the horrors and self-inflicted tragedies of the human race, from the dawn of historical time to the present day, and yet as a counterpoint to all of that, we can say: *But we gave birth to God*. A great writer once said, "History is a nightmare from which I am trying to awake."* But today's gospel tells us that the seeming nightmare of history is really just the surface. Beneath that, the deepest reality of history is a story of promise and fulfill-

---

* James Joyce, *Ulysses* (New York: Vintage Books, 1986), 28.

ment. Pessimism is ultimately superficial. Christmas is the real meaning of all of human history.

Of course, this meaning is not always obvious but mostly hidden. All those people mentioned in the genealogy we just heard did not go around thinking or saying, "Let me beget an ancestor to the Incarnate God." They went about their lives, doing and suffering and sinning. But they lived and died in faith—as we just heard in our epistle reading—trusting that somehow God's promises would come to fulfillment, and praying that somehow their lives would contribute to that fulfillment. But they could never have imagined that this fulfillment would be nothing less than God's becoming human in order to make us divine and that their names would one day be recited among the human ancestors of God.

But what about us? Now that God has come in the flesh, what are we supposed to do? Is there nothing left for us to do except wait for the end of the world and remind ourselves that God came into the world sometime in the middle of history? Of course not! God's coming into the world and God's becoming flesh only began with the birth of Jesus and we have been called to bring this work to completion. The eternal Word and Son of the Father became flesh in the child Jesus some two thousand years ago, but his plan is to become flesh in the whole human race, to gather us all up and sanctify us and glorify us as members of his body. He continues this work now as he sits in glory at the right hand of the Father. Each one of us is called to participate in this work until it comes to completion.

We do not know at what point God, in his inscrutable wisdom, will deem that our human contribution to this work has come to a suitable completion. Just like no one could have known before the birth of Christ when the preparation of God's people would have reached the point when it would be fitting, from God's point of view, for the Word to become flesh. And we do not know exactly how all our workings and sufferings contribute to the completion of God's plan for uniting all things in himself. Just as we do not know the day and the hour when the Son of Man will come in his glory, we do not know exactly how everything we do in faith contributes to the coming of that day and that hour. But in faith we live as strangers and foreigners on this earth and we look forward to the city "whose architect and builder is God," who has also called us to participate, through his grace, in the building of that heavenly city.

So, until that day comes, we have to make use of the present time to prepare for its coming. We know what we have to do to prepare for this coming: We have to repent of everything that is contrary to God's will as shown forth in Christ, remembering the exhortation of St. Paul that God's patience is meant to lead us to repentance. We have to proclaim the gospel in season and out of season, remembering that God, in his gracious mercy, has ordained that before he comes to judge all the world, "the gospel must first be proclaimed to all the nations." We have to continue the revolution that Christ has already begun with his coming by sharing in his work of showing the strength of his mercy, of bringing down the powerful from their thrones and lifting up the lowly, of filling the hungry with good things.

If we do all these things, then despite all the signs around us of human failure, we can exult and rejoice and participate in the great success of our human race, which is to give birth to God, to merge our human life with his divine life. By faith, we know that God who has begun this great good work in us will bring it to completion. By his grace, he has granted that we may have a share in helping

Eph. 1:10

Matt. 24:36

Heb. 11:10

Rom. 2:4

2 Tim. 4:2

Mark 13:10

Luke 1:52–53

Phil. 1:6

to bring this great work of his incarnation and our deification to completion.

As we look forward to the great feast of Christmas in
which we celebrate the beginning of this work of the union
in the flesh of God and humanity, we also look forward to
the completion of this work when Christ comes to judge the
world and "hand over the kingdom to God his Father."   *1 Cor. 15:24*

Since we have such a hope and such promises, let us
now approach the holy table and partake of the spiritual
food and drink that cleanses us from all defilement of flesh
and spirit and makes us into a "people prepared" for the   *2 Cor. 7:1*
Lord's coming—prepared to rejoice without ceasing in   *Luke 1:17*
his first coming in the flesh, and prepared to receive him
with endless joy at his second coming in glory, through
the grace of our Lord Jesus Christ, the love of God the
Father, and the communion of the Holy Spirit. Amen.

The Birthday of God

Galatians 4:4–7; Matthew 2:1–12

Brothers and sisters who are dearly beloved in Christ Jesus our Lord:

> Christ is born; Glorify him!
> *Al-maseeh wulidah; fa majiduh!*
> *Cristo ha nacido; Glorificále!*
> *Christos Rozhdayet'sya; Slavite Yoho!*
> *Christos gennetai; doxasate!**

Brothers and sisters, today, despite snowstorms and all the troubles and calamities that constantly afflict our human race, there is nevertheless great and irrepressible

---

* It is a Byzantine tradition to exchange the greeting "Christ is born; Glorify him!" throughout the Christmas season, beginning with the Christmas liturgy. The above greetings correspond to the native languages of various members of the congregation to whom this homily was delivered: English, Arabic, Spanish, and Ukrainian, ending with the traditional Greek. This homily was preached at a Christmas liturgy that was celebrated in the immediate aftermath of a major snowstorm, to which I allude in the following paragraph.

joy and exultation in both heaven and earth. In heaven, all
the angelic choirs sing today the glory of the One who is
"transcendent in essence" but who emptied himself and
became a little child in order to make us true children of
God.* And all over the earth, people in every kind of condition—the rich and the poor; the sick and the healthy;
men, women, and children—all celebrate together today
the birth of the One who was rich in his divinity but became poor for our sakes, the One who is strong in his
divinity but made himself weak in order to bear all our
diseases, the eternal God who became a man born of a
woman, and even a little child.

Phil. 2:7

2 Cor. 8:9

Matt. 8:17

    Everywhere we look today, wherever our mind turns
and whatever our senses observe, we find reason to in-
crease our joy in this glorious feast. If we think of all the
goodness of the world—the bounties of nature and the
kindness that human beings sometimes show one another—we rejoice in celebrating today the perfect union
of all heavenly and earthly goodness in the human birth
of the One who is the eternally begotten Son and perfect
image of the Father's goodness. If we attend to all the evil
and sadness in the world, we still rejoice in celebrating
today the birth of the One who takes away all the sin and
evil of the world, the One who has conquered death and
who grants us eternal life, the Bridegroom who has come
to inaugurate the great wedding feast of the marriage of
heaven and earth. Today, indeed, for all who keep this glo-

John 1:29

* The quoted phrase is from a prescribed hymn ("kontakion") for
the Christmas liturgy: "Today the Virgin gives birth to the Transcendent
in Essence, and the earth presents a cave to the Inaccessible. The angels
with the shepherds sing his glory, and the Wise Men with the star travel
on their way, for to us is born a New Child, who is God from all eternity."
December Menaion, Service Books of the Byzantine Churches (Boston:
Sophia Press, 1990), 337.

rious feast, joy reigns supreme, in wonderful fulfillment of the announcement of the angel, "I am bringing you good *Luke 2:10* news of great joy for all the people."

Now, of all the ways that we can describe the reason for our joy today—the reason for the joy of this feast— the simplest one is the best: today, we are celebrating the birthday of God! Hopefully, all of us have experienced the joy of celebrating the birthday of someone we love. But today, we are experiencing the fullness of joy because we are celebrating the birthday of the One who loved us into being, the One who is Love himself. So, we can also say that we are celebrating today the birthday of Love.

Of course, someone could say that in fact God doesn't have a birthday, because God always existed and always exists. God is eternal and did not begin to be at any time. So, there is no such thing as a birthday of God. Perhaps there is a clever philosopher among us who will want to raise such an objection. But, in fact, the premise of this objection is not completely true, but a half-truth at best. It is true that God is eternal and there is no beginning to God's existence. But it is also true, and much more completely and wonderfully true, that God the Father eternally gives birth to God the Son by sharing his whole divine life with the Son from all eternity to all eternity. And so, there is an eternal birthday in God, the eternal birth of God from God, Light from Light, true God from true God. From all eternity to all eternity, there is a never-ending divine celebration of the birthday of the eternal begetting of the Son from the Father, in the joy of the Holy Spirit.

Gal. 4:4 Today, my brothers and sisters, we are celebrating the glorious mystery that, in the fullness of time, God chose to celebrate this eternal birthday on earth, by adding a second birthday to this first and eternal birthday of the eternal begetting of the Son from the Father. The only begotten

Son, eternally begotten of his divine Father, was born in our world of a human mother. As we read in our epistle, God has chosen to do this in order that we, who were born under the law of servitude to God, would become adopted as children of God through the human birth of the eternal Son of God. By joining his eternal birth from the Father to a human birth, our Lord Jesus Christ gives us a new and divine birth, in which we are "born not of blood or of the will of the flesh or of the will of man, but of God." *John 1:13*

Today, the joy that we have in celebrating this great mystery of our salvation is made even greater when we consider the significance of the glorious fact that God chose to manifest his divinity as a little child. God became a baby. And, in doing so, God manifested to us his eternal baby-ness. In the troparion for today's feast, we sing, "Thy Nativity, O Christ our God, has shed the light of knowledge upon the world." One of the most wonderful rays of the light of knowledge that our Lord's nativity has shed upon this world is the knowledge of God's eternal baby-ness. When we speak of God's eternal baby-ness, we are declaring the great mystery of the incomprehensible grandeur of God's humility, the unfathomable meekness of his greatness, the inscrutable gentleness of his infinite power.

We can glimpse this mystery by thinking of human babies. When a new baby is born, the whole household becomes centered on the needs of the baby. Everything is organized around what the baby needs and what the baby wants. Everyone wants to hold the baby and adore it. The new baby, in a real sense, becomes the boss of the whole house. But a new baby rules over the household not by orders and threats but by weakness and vulnerability, not by forcibly imposing his or her will on us but by drawing out our love. God became a baby in order to manifest to us the mystery that he wishes to rule the world in just this way, in a childlike and baby-like way. God wanted to rule his creation not as a tyrant king who forces us to follow his laws, by threats and compulsion, but as a helpless child who draws out our love by his weakness. God became a baby because he wanted to hand himself over completely into our hands. He who holds heaven and earth in the palms of his hands wanted human beings not to grovel at his feet, so to speak, with fear and trembling, but to hold him in their arms with loving and careful adoration. And so, my brothers and sisters, on this wonderful feast, we are offered the grace to welcome anew the baby-ness of God. Through this feast, we are called to recognize the awesome mystery that God has chosen to depend on each one of us as much as a newborn baby depends on its parents. God wants to depend on us as much as we depend on him. He wants us to feed him with the virtues that he himself grants us, to clothe him with the holiness that comes from him, to love him with the love through which he created us and saved us.

Today's gospel tells us that when the star that was leading the magi to the child Jesus stopped, they were overwhelmed with joy, and when they saw him they *Matt. 2:10* knelt down and worshipped. Today, the star of the liturgical year has stopped for us at this great feast in which we celebrate the birth of the only begotten Son of God as a human baby. Like the magi, we are overwhelmed with joy. Let us also be like the magi in bending the knees of our hearts and worshipping this newborn child who is eternally begotten of the Father. Let us also be like Mary and Joseph in our dedication to feeding this child, whose *John 4:34* food is to draw all people into doing the will of the Father. Let us also give this child the drink that he needs, since he *John 19:28* constantly thirsts for the salvation of all humanity. Let us also keep in mind that this very child, who depends on us for his food and drink, is the same one who will sit at the awesome judgment seat at the end of time, and say to us that he considers whatever food and drink and kindness we have granted to our fellow human beings as food and drink and kindness granted to him.

Matt. 25:40

My brothers and sisters, the Gospel of St. Luke tells us that the parents of the newborn Jesus placed him in a manger because there was no room for them at the inn. A manger, of course, is a feeding box for animals. But instead of earthly food for animals, that manger in Bethlehem contained the bread that transforms our animal nature into a divine nature, the bread that came down from heaven to grant eternal life to all the world. Today, this holy altar will bear the same content as that manger. After the eucharistic consecration, the same bread of life that was lying in that manger will be present on this altar. The same life that animated the body and blood of the child Jesus will be present and active in the bread and wine that will be consecrated on this altar. May our eating of this heavenly bread enable us to feed the One who is our true Bread. And may our drinking from the cup on this altar enable us to quench the thirst of the One who is the fountain of life. And may the grace of this holy feast enable us to welcome and nurture the Christ-child within us until we reach the measure of the full stature of the risen and glorified Christ, to whom we ascribe glory and honor and adoration, along with his eternal Father, and their all-holy, good, and life-giving Spirit, now and always and forever and ever. Amen.

John 6:51

Ps. 36:9

Eph. 4:13

THEOPHANY

Baptism into
Trinitarian Life

Titus 2:11–14; 3:4–7; Matthew 3:13–17

My brothers and sisters who are dearly beloved in Christ Jesus our Lord:

It is the way of the Lord to refresh the weary, feed the hungry, and lift up the downtrodden. That is also the way of the liturgical year, which applies to the rhythm of our lives the benevolence and loving-kindness of the Lord. So it is that in the middle of winter, as the daylight of this earth is shortened, we are granted the grace of celebrating the birth of the Everlasting Day into the short days of our lives.* Even though it might be cold and dreary

---

While Western Christians celebrate the feast of Epiphany on January 6, which focuses primarily on the magi's visit to the infant Jesus, the Eastern celebration of Theophany on the same date focuses on Jesus's baptism as a manifestation of the divine Trinity—hence, "theophany," or in Greek, *theophaneia*, meaning "divine manifestation." It is fair to say that the feast of Theophany is granted considerably greater prominence in Byzantine piety than is the Western commemoration of Epiphany.

* This is an echo of the wording of St. Augustine: "Let us celebrate the festal day on which the great and eternal Day came from the great and eternal Day into this short temporal day of ours." Sermon 185.2.

outside, we bask in the new warmth that the bright Sun of Righteousness has brought into our world that had been darkened by sin.

It is also the way of human beings that we quickly forget the great works and gifts of the Lord, and go back to our grumbling and complaining and wondering where is God and why isn't he helping us. But then the Lord responds to our complaints and our forgetfulness with even more gifts, bestowing on us from the fullness of his love grace upon grace. So, following the great grace of the celebration of Christmas, we are now granted the equally wonderful grace of the celebration of this great feast of Theophany.

In this feast, we celebrate the manifestation of the Holy Trinity, as we sing in the troparion:*

> At your baptism in the Jordan, O Lord, the worship of the Trinity was revealed. For the Father's voice bore witness to you by calling you his Beloved Son. And the Spirit, in the form of a dove, confirmed the truth of these words. O Christ God, who have appeared to us and enlightened the world, glory to You.**

Perhaps we don't think much about the Holy Trinity, or we think that this is a mystery beyond our comprehension. We can't understand it, so we think it's okay to just forget about it. But in the Christian faith, a mystery is not something that is okay to forget about. A mystery, in our Christian faith, is a reality that we live out and that pervades and transforms our lives, even if we don't completely understand it.

---

* In the Byzantine liturgy, a "troparion" is a short hymn. Every feast day is celebrated by its own "troparion" that highlights the theme of the feast.

** *January Menaion*, Service Books of the Byzantine Churches (Boston: Sophia Press, 2003), 190.

In this feast, we are given the grace not so much to understand or figure out the Trinity, but rather to experience our own immersion in the life of the Holy Trinity. Our immersion into the life of the Trinity takes place through Jesus's immersion into the waters of the Jordan. When Jesus immersed himself in the waters of the Jordan, he immersed himself into the condition of our sinfulness, in solidarity with us. But, at the same time, he immersed us into the life of the Trinity.

When Jesus came to John to undergo the baptism of repentance, he was not of course repenting for his own sins, since he was completely without sin. But he entered into the condition of our sinfulness, and took all the weight of our sins upon himself, and repented on our behalf.* Therefore, in him, our repentance is perfected and the way is opened for us to be taken into the life of the Holy Trinity. Because Jesus stood in solidarity with us in our sinfulness and offered repentance on our behalf, we stand in solidarity with him in his perfect communion with the Father and the Spirit. This means that everyone of us is present in him, when Jesus hears the voice of the Father saying, "This is my beloved Son, with whom I am well pleased." And the Holy Spirit rests on each one of us when he rests on Jesus.

Matt. 3:17

Matt. 3:16

This is what we celebrate today: our entrance into the life of the Trinity. St. Paul tells us: "Your life is hidden with Christ in God." But if our life is hidden with Christ in God, it is hidden in the Holy Trinity, who is the one and only true God. And even if it is hidden from the sight of all the world, it is not completely hidden from the eyes

Col. 3:3

---

* For a fuller and more detailed exposition of this point, see K. Anatolios, *Deification through the Cross: An Eastern Christian Theology of Salvation* (Grand Rapids: Eerdmans, 2020), esp. 151–59.

of our faith, which enables us to hear the voice of the Father calling us his beloved children and to experience the power of the Spirit resting on us and leading us.

When we do the Great Blessing of the Waters, and when we drink of this blessed water, this mystery is revealed to us again and impressed into our soul and body and spirit. Through the power of the sacrament, this water which we are about to bless is the very same water, having the same spiritual power as the water in which Jesus was baptized and which Jesus transformed by his baptism. When we bless this water, it becomes transfigured by the power of Christ and permeated with Christ's victory over sin and death. It becomes, as we shall say in the prayers of the blessing, a "fountain of incorruptibility, a gift of sanctification, a remission of sins, a healing medicine for illness, a destroyer of evils."*

This does not mean it becomes a magic potion, so that as soon as we drink this water, our troubles will disappear. Remember: After Jesus's own baptism, what does he do and what happens to him? He doesn't retire to Florida and meditate on the beach. He is led by the Spirit into the desert to be tempted by the devil. But he is victorious in this temptation and then sets out to fulfill the salvation of all the world and to bring the whole world back into the embrace of the Holy Trinity.

When we come to drink this water, then, we are not magically wiping out all our sorrows and sufferings. But what we are doing is letting the Lord Jesus plunge himself deep into our sufferings, just as he did in the Jordan River, and we are also letting him take us, with all our sufferings, into the life of the Holy Trinity.

* *The Festal Menaion*, trans. Mother Mary and Archimandrite Kallistos Ware (South Canaan, PA: St. Tikhon's Seminary Press, 1998), 357 (altered).

So, my brothers and sisters, as we come forward to receive this water and drink from it after it has been blessed, what we are promised is not a magic escape from our sufferings, but rather Christ's victorious solidarity with us in our sufferings, in the midst of our sinfulness and our many temptations. We are receiving the power to use our sufferings to be in communion with the death of Christ that we may also share in his resurrection. Above all, we are receiving the power to always hear the voice of the Father resounding mystically in our hearts, "You are my beloved son, my beloved daughter. I am well pleased with you." And we are receiving the power of the Holy Spirit, resting upon us and leading us to victory over every temptation and anything that threatens to separate us from the love of God in Christ Jesus.

Rom. 8:39

So, let us now come forward eagerly to receive the body and blood of the Lord and then let us plunge with him into the waters of the Jordan and into the glorious life of the Holy Trinity, which is revealed to us and in us through the awesome mysteries we celebrate today, by the wonderful grace of the Father, the Son, and the Holy Spirit. Amen.

THE MANIFESTATION
OF CHRISTIAN GLORY

Titus 2:11–14; 3:4–7; Matthew 3:13–17

My brothers and sisters who are dearly beloved in Christ Jesus our Lord:

It is perhaps a little bit jarring—at least, I always find it a little bit jarring myself—to move so quickly, as we do in the Byzantine calendar, from the birthday of Christ to the feast of Theophany. Less than two weeks ago, we celebrated Christmas and now we celebrate the baptism of Christ as a full-grown man, and the revelation of the Holy Trinity through his baptism, and the beginning of Jesus's public ministry.

The Western calendar makes the transition easier by focusing its celebration of Epiphany on the baby Jesus and the visit of the magi, representing the recognition of the Messiah by the Gentiles. But the Byzantine calendar doesn't see any problem with this rapid transition from focusing on the birth of Christ to focusing on the revelation of the Trinity through the adult Christ. In fact, it draws our attention to it, as you will hear in the beautiful prayers of the blessing of the waters, in which the priest says: "In the preceding feast, we saw you as a child, while in the present, we behold you full-grown, our God made manifest, perfect God from perfect God."*

One of the graces, I believe, of this quick transition is that it highlights how closely intertwined are two fundamental aspects of the Christian life: hiddenness and manifestation, the Nazareth hiddenness of Christmas and the open manifestation of the Jordan theophany.

In the feast of Christmas, the eternal Son of God, through whom all things were created, comes to be born in a little cave, because there was no room for him at the inn. And then he grows in his humanity, at the same rate as any other human being, without giving any public demonstration of his divinity, his divine life being hidden within his humanity, the Word of God resounding within a human silence. This aspect of Nazareth hiddenness is a fundamental element of our Christian life. St. Paul tells us that our lives are "hidden with Christ in God." And Jesus himself tells us that our life in the kingdom of God is like a mustard seed that is the smallest of all the seeds but then grows slowly, and seemingly imperceptibly, until it becomes a large tree, and the birds of the air come to nest in it.

Col. 3:3

Matt. 13:31–32

But this aspect of Nazareth hiddenness is always intertwined in our Christian life with that of Jordan theophany, and it is the latter aspect that we celebrate today. When we celebrate the theophany of the Lord in the Jordan, we recognize that while our lives are hidden with Christ in God, God himself is not hidden from us but has fully disclosed himself to us in Christ, in the full splendor of his saving

---

* *The Festal Menaion*, trans. Mother Mary and Archimandrite Kallistos Ware (South Canaan, PA: St. Tikhon's Seminary Press, 1998), 354 (altered).

glory. In this glorious feast of Theophany, we experience the fulfillment of the prophecy of Isaiah, who said:

Isa. 30:19–21, 26

> Truly, O people in Zion, inhabitants of Jerusalem, you shall weep no more ... your Teacher will not hide himself anymore, but your eyes shall see your Teacher. And when you turn to the right or when you turn to the left, your ears shall hear a word behind you, saying, "This is the way, walk in it." ... Moreover the light of the moon will be like the light of the sun, and the light of the sun will be sevenfold, like the light of seven days, on the day the Lord binds up the injuries of the people and heals the wounds inflicted [on them].

Indeed, my brothers and sisters, today our Lord and Teacher no longer hides himself, but our eyes see the fullness of his splendor. Today, the heavens are opened for us and we see the glory of the only begotten Son to whom the Father bears witness, saying, "This is my beloved Son, in whom I am well pleased." And we see the Spirit of God descend upon him, in the form of a dove, proclaiming the fullness of peace between heaven and earth.

And so today, we celebrate, first of all and above all, the manifestation of the Holy Trinity, as we sing in the troparion: "At your baptism in the Jordan, O Lord, the worship of the Trinity was revealed." Today, the Holy Trinity is not manifested to us merely as a spectacle, or as a bit of information that we are given but can't understand. Rather, the Holy Trinity is manifested to us as the *life* in which we live

Acts 17:28

and move and have our being. Through our participation in Christ, by sharing in the baptism with which he was baptized for us, each of us can hear the Father's voice saying to us, "You are my beloved son, my beloved daughter, you who have become a member of the body of my eter-

nal beloved Son." Through our participation in Christ, by
sharing in the baptism with which he was baptized for us,
the Spirit of God descends upon us and fills us with the
peace of God that passes all understanding.   *Phil. 4:7*

It is only this fullness of participation in the life of
the Holy Trinity that brings to fulfillment the promise
of the psalmist: "He will make your vindication shine like
the light, and the justice of your cause like the noonday."   *Ps. 37:6*
We can have no more vindication than to hear the Father's
voice saying, "You are my beloved son; you are my beloved
daughter." The justice of our cause now shines like the light
because the eternal radiance of the Father's light has en-   *Heb. 1:3*
tered into our chaos and sin and become for us our justice,
our righteousness, our sanctification, and redemption.

The prophecy of Isaiah also promised: "When you   *1 Cor. 1:30*
turn to the right or when you turn to the left, your ears
shall hear a word behind you, saying, 'This is the way, walk
in it.'" Today, this "way" in which we are to walk is fully
revealed to us as the way of Christ's death and resurrection. This is the way that Christ manifested by accepting
the baptism of repentance offered by John, on our behalf.
In this way, he accepts to enter into our sin and death, and
to drown them in the waters of the Jordan, and to rise up
as the new Adam who frees us from the bondage of sin.
And so, we had a special prayer in our litany today: "That
the fruits of holy baptism may be realized in us, and that
we may partake of the death of Christ our God, in order
to partake of his Resurrection, let us pray to the Lord."

It is in this spirit, and with this understanding, that we
bless and receive the holy water today, which becomes
for us, by sacramental grace, identical with the water of
the Jordan River that was sanctified by the baptism of
Christ. We receive this holy water, to bless ourselves with
it and to drink from it, not as some magical potion that

will take away any sickness or difficulty, but in order to unite ourselves, and our whole lives, with the death and resurrection of Christ.

Finally, the prophecy of Isaiah talks about the beauty of creation that becomes fully manifest and perfected by the beauty of salvation: In that day, he says, "the light of the moon will be like the light of the sun, and the light of the sun will be sevenfold, like the light of seven days, on the day the Lord binds up the injuries of the people and heals the wounds inflicted [on them]." Likewise, the prayers for the blessing of the waters, which we are about to proclaim at the end of this liturgy, exult in the beauty of the creation that is being healed and sanctified by the saving glory of Christ's theophany:

> Today, the world is filled with splendor by the
>   light of the Lord.
> Today, the moon shines upon the world with
>   the brightness of its rays.
> Today the glittering stars make the inhab-
>   ited earth fair with the radiance of their
>   shining . . .
> Today, earth and sea share the joy of the world,
>   and the world is filled with gladness.*

All this is manifested for us today, my brothers and sisters, as we celebrate the great Feast of Theophany: the glorious life of the Holy Trinity in which we ourselves find true life and the love that vindicates our existence; the way of Christ's death and resurrection that grants us saving righteousness and sanctification; and the renewed and perfected beauty of all creation.

* *Festal Menaion*, 354–55 (altered).

It is true that our lives are still hidden with Christ in God; much of our lives are still permeated by the quietness and obscurity of Nazareth; and, certainly here in South Bend, the beauties of nature are also largely hidden from us in these winter months. But, at the very same time, by the grace of the feast we celebrate today, through this quietness we can hear the voice of the Lord resounding over the waters, the living waters that flow out of our hearts through the Holy Spirit who has been given to us; in the midst of obscurity, the very life of God is broken open for us; in these cloudy days, the sun of righteousness shines brightly upon us, "more brightly than the light of seven days," with the brightness of the everlasting day of the risen Christ.

Ps. 29:1

John 7:38

Isa. 30:26

Indeed, my brothers and sisters, the grace of God our Savior has appeared to us. Let us now eat and drink of this grace of our Lord Jesus Christ, and the love of God the Father, in the communion of the Holy Spirit. Amen.

Titus 2:11

LET US BAPTIZE CHRIST!

Titus 2:11–14; 3:4–7; Matthew 3:13–17

My brothers and sisters who are dearly beloved in Christ Jesus our Lord:

The apostle Paul says to us in his letter to the Colossians, "When Christ who is your life appears, then you also will appear with him in glory." In that context, he was likely speaking of Christ's appearance at the end of history, when this present world will give way to the fulfillment of the kingdom of God. But the Lord himself has told us that to us, his disciples, the secrets of the kingdom have already been revealed. Among these secrets, which the world does not know but which have been revealed to us, is the appearance of the Lord's glory that we celebrate on this great feast of Theophany.

The word "theophany," as many of you know, is the English form of the Greek word *theophaneia*, which means "appearance of God." Today, we celebrate the appearance of Jesus as God, as one of the Holy Trinity, as the eternal beloved Son of the Father with whom the Father is eternally well pleased, as the One on whom the Holy Spirit eternally rests and remains, and the One who gives us the Spirit.

Col. 3:4

But on this great feast, we also celebrate our appearance with him in glory. Today, we recognize the appearance of Christ as our very Life—"When Christ who is *your life* appears, you also will appear with him in glory." Since we have been baptized into Christ, we have put on Christ, as we chanted in the antiphon, and the life of Christ, all the power of Christ's life and every moment of it that he lived both in the flesh and after his ascension into heaven, has become our life. Henceforth, as the apostle Paul also said, our life is hidden with Christ in God.   *Col. 3:3*

Our life in Christ may be hidden from the world but it should not be hidden from us, who have put on this life through baptism. On this glorious feast of the Theophany of Christ, not only does Christ appear to us in glory, but our own life also appears to us in glory. The secret glory of our lives, hidden from us through our spiritual forgetfulness and inattention, is revealed to us today and appears to us within the glory of the Holy Trinity. Within that appearance of the glory of our own lives hidden in God, each one of us can mystically hear the voice of the Father saying to us, "You are my beloved son; you are my beloved daughter; I delight in you with the same delight in which I am well-pleased with my only begotten Son." Within that manifestation of our life in Christ, we recognize that we   *1 Cor. 6:19* are temples of the Holy Spirit and the dwelling place of divine glory.

But in today's feast, we do not merely receive a vision of the glory of Christ and of our glory in Christ. Through sacramental grace, we receive the power to integrate our whole lives into that vision. And the key to this power is revealed to us in the gospel reading for today's feast. This key, which is given to us through the grace of our baptism into Christ, is the very same power that was given to John the Baptist, the forerunner of our Lord: *the power to baptize Christ.*

Yes, I know that it sounds strange to say that. We know—because the gospel tells us so—that it seemed very strange for John the Baptist when Jesus approached him and asked to be baptized by him. John was flustered and embarrassed and confused by this request. After all, he was preaching and performing a baptism of repentance and people were coming to him "confessing their sins." When the religious leaders, the Pharisees and Sadducees, came to him to receive this baptism of repentance, and he suspected that they were doing this just for the sake of appearance and without sincerity, he scolded them, "You brood of vipers. Who warned you to flee from the wrath of *Matt. 3:7–8*   God? Bear fruit worthy of repentance." He also said to the people, "I baptize you with water for repentance, but one who is more powerful than I is coming after me; I am not worthy to carry his sandals. He will baptize you with the *Matt. 3:11*   Holy Spirit and with fire." But now, here was the very same One, the only Sinless One who takes away the sin of the world, lining up with sinners who were confessing their sins, to receive from John a baptism of repentance.

Imagine if you heard that someone had a vision of Christ lining up in a confession line, waiting to go to confession. That would seem like a weird vision and I am sure that it would be met with suspicion. But this was not just a vision that John the Baptist had; it was the reality. So, understandably, he was confused and scandalized and the evangelist Matthew tells us that he tried to prevent Jesus from being baptized by him, saying, "I need to be baptized *Matt. 3:14*   by you, and do you come to me?"

Matthew continues: "But Jesus answered him, 'Let it be so now, for it is proper for us in this way to fulfill all *Matt. 3:15*   righteousness.' Then John consented." He consented, but I doubt if John the Baptist understood what Jesus meant. He consented just because he knew that Jesus was the

Lord and Messiah and that he should do whatever Jesus told him to do, whether he understood it or not.

But the full revelation of what Jesus meant by undergoing a baptism of repentance and how that would "fulfill all righteousness" was only made manifest after Jesus's death and resurrection. Then, it became clear that the way that Jesus chose to take away the sins of the world was by bearing them sinlessly in himself, by being in complete solidarity with sinners, not by sinning with them but by taking on the consequences of their sin and offering a perfect repentance on their behalf. This is the way that Christ chose to "fulfill all righteousness," and when he rose from the dead, he became our righteousness, and gave us the power to die to sin and to live in God through him.

1 Cor. 1:30

But all this would not have been possible if John had succeeded in preventing Jesus from undergoing a baptism of repentance in solidarity with sinners. In asking John to baptize him, Jesus was asking John to let him take his place among sinners so that he could carry their sins and dissolve them in his own righteousness, so that the heavens can open up for us and the glory of the Holy Trinity can be revealed to us and we can become the dwelling place of divine glory.

In a similar way, my brothers and sisters, Jesus is asking each of us today to baptize him—and not just today, but every day and in every situation. We have been baptized in him once and for all, and we do not need to be baptized in him more than once. Once we are baptized in him, he lives in us and offers us all the riches of his divinized humanity. But because his life in us does not take away our freedom, he always asks us to accept his solidarity with us and waits for our permission—he waits for this permission every day and in every situation.

He is continually asking to be in solidarity with our afflictions, our tribulations, our sinfulness, our misery, our terror. And in asking to be in solidarity with us in all these troubled waters of our lives, he is asking to be baptized by us and in us. He is asking for permission to plunge into the depths of our sinfulness and suffering so that he can become our righteousness, our sanctification, and our glory, so that in the midst of all our suffering and sinfulness, we can always hear in him the Father's voice, "You are my beloved son; you are my beloved daughter. Rejoice in the Spirit of my love."

So, my brothers and sisters in Christ, on this feast of the Lord's baptism, let us not only contemplate the baptism of Christ; let us make sure to baptize Christ into our lives right now, into the very present moment of our lives with all its difficulties and tribulations. Let us permit Christ to plunge into the depths of the miseries of our lives so that the heavens may be opened up for us. Let the whole world be made new for us as we allow Christ to put to death in us whatever belongs to the sinful oldness of this world whose form is passing away before our very eyes.

May the holy body and precious blood of our Lord and God and Savior, Jesus Christ, of which we are about to partake, enable us to continually baptize into our lives the One whose baptism for our sake has put to death our sin and transported us into the fullness of the glory of the Father, the Son, and the Holy Spirit. Amen.

LENT, PART 1

THE ICONOGRAPHY OF
CHRISTIAN DISCIPLESHIP

Hebrews 11:24–26, 32–40; 12:1–2; John 1:43–51

My brothers and sisters who are dearly beloved in Christ Jesus our Lord:

A despondent person once said, "The sun also rises and the sun goes down. . . . All things are wearisome more than one can express. . . . What has been is what will be, and what has been done is what will be done; there is nothing new under the sun."

Eccles. 1:5, 8–9

Now, here in South Bend, we might want to say, "*If only the sun would rise and go down on a regular basis.*" Nevertheless, as winter drags on and outwears any welcome we might have initially granted it, and as we continue our slog through the school year, and as we withstand the daily reports of the atrocities of our human race and struggle to find a convincing counter-witness in our own hearts, we can certainly identify with the weariness of the author of Ecclesiastes: "All things are wearisome more than one can express."

But our good and loving God, the Father of mercy and
the source of every good and perfect gift, has granted us
the great gift of the liturgical year as an antidote to this
weariness. By fully sharing with us his Son and his Spirit,
he has made all things new with an indestructible newness
that can never fade, and he has distributed this wonderful
newness in the midst of the drudgery of our weariness
through the seasons of the liturgical year.

James 1:17

Of all these seasons, we are now embarking on the
greatest one, the one most full of splendor and light and
newness of life, the paschal season, beginning with Great
Lent and leading to the glorious feasts of the resurrection
of Christ, his ascension into heaven, and the pouring out
of the Holy Spirit upon us.

Today, we celebrate the first Sunday of this season of
Great Lent, the Sunday of Orthodoxy. On this day, we re-
affirm the veneration of icons, as originally proclaimed by
the seventh ecumenical council in AD 787. It seems to me
that one important aspect of the fittingness of beginning
Great Lent in this way is that Great Lent is a time not only
to venerate the "images" of our Lord and the saints—the
word "icon" means "image"—but to renew ourselves as
images and icons of God. What the Byzantine tradition is
telling us, I think, is that during the season of Great Lent,
each one of us is called to become an iconographer of our
very selves. Each of us has the task of working on the icon
that is ourselves, cooperating with God's grace in renewing the image of God within us. This is how we begin this
season of great renewal, leading up to the glorious feast of
the Resurrection of Christ, by getting to work on renewing the image of God within us, following the instructions
of St. Paul when he told us to "strip off the old self with its
practices and clothe yourselves with the new self, which is
being renewed in knowledge according to the image—the
icon—of its creator."

Col. 3:9–10

So, how do we do this, practically speaking? Well, to-day's gospel gives us our first lesson in this program of self-iconography. Let's go over some of the main points of this lesson.

At the beginning of today's gospel, we hear two words that are the key to this whole Lenten program of renewing the image of God within us, two words that are the source of all newness, all joy, all confidence and peace and con-solation, for every Christian. These are the words of Jesus to Philip: "Follow me." None of us would be here today if we had not at some point in our lives heard, deep in our hearts and souls, these beautiful and life-giving words, spoken by the eternal Word: "Follow me."

We begin our program of self-iconography, then, by hearing these words again, by relishing these words, by rejoicing in these words, by letting these words be more precious to us than any other words, by letting these words sustain us more than any earthly food and drink, by repeating these words to ourselves day and night: "Follow me." Let us pray for the grace of hearing these words with ever-greater volume and depth and intensity throughout this holy season, so that we can follow our Lord through death to the indestructible newness of resurrection life.

Jesus's encounter with Nathanael gives us yet more valuable lessons for the Lenten program of paschal self-iconography. This encounter is one of those beautiful lit-tle conversations that we find in the Gospels in which so much depth and warmth of intimacy is exchanged through just a few words. Jesus greets Nathanael with this myste-rious praise: "Here is a true Israelite in whom there is no guile." We are not told why Jesus said this about Nathanael or what exactly he meant by it. But, clearly, the guileless-ness of Nathanael—whatever that was—was something that immediately resonated with Jesus; it was something that was key to the immediate intensity and warmth of the connection between Jesus and Nathanael.

As we try to imagine what Jesus could have meant by saying that Nathanael was a man without guile, we should start by thinking how full of guile and deceit are our own lives. All the posturing and pretending and strategizing about how we appear to others is just so much guile and deceit, even if it is not outright lying. At the same time, we let ourselves be deceived and beguiled by all kinds of distractions, by all kinds of inauthenticity. We also deceive ourselves by hiding from our true selves, with all the darkness and terror and pain that may be hidden there, and by conforming ourselves to the images that the world projects rather than the true image of God within us. All this guile, all this deception that we both make and suffer, what a great and oppressive burden it all is! It's like so much dead weight that covers over and hides our authentic selves that were made in the image of God and that Christ wants to renew in us.

Lent is the time to take off that dead weight. Lent can be our vacation from guile, a vacation from the strenuous and wearisome constant laboring in the arts of deception. The demons of deception and guile can only be exorcised by heartfelt prayer and fasting, and this is what we are called to this Lent, my brothers and sisters.

But there is still more we can learn from Nathanael about what it means to be without guile. As I said, the gospel does not explain to us why Jesus said of Nathanael that he is a man without guile, or what exactly that means. But I think that it does give us two little hints, which can also be valuable lessons for attaining guilelessness for ourselves, as part of our Lent program of self-iconography. An important element of guilelessness is simply knowing ourselves, as we are, without pretense, with all our hopes and fears and pains. There are two ways in which Nathanael shows us how this kind of guilelessness determines our relationship to Jesus.

In the first place, it seems to me that it was part of Nathanael's guilelessness and transparency that he was in touch with an inner desperation, a searching and hoping for God's deliverance, for a decisive intervention by God himself. He was looking and hoping for the Messiah, the King of Israel. I think that this is indicated in the gospel by the fact that Philip immediately goes to Nathanael after he meets Jesus and he says to Nathanael, "We have found the one about whom Moses in the law and also the prophets wrote, Jesus of Nazareth." I don't think that Philip would have gone immediately to Nathanael and told him this if he did not know that this was something that Nathanael was concerned about. This must have been something that they had had previous conversations about. They were both looking for the one whom Philip now says that he has found. So Nathanael, in his guilelessness, in his transparency to himself, was aware of this desperate *hope* for salvation.

At the same time, another aspect of Nathanael's guilelessness is that he was also in touch with his own hopelessness and despair and skepticism. So, when Philip says to him, "We have found the Messiah," he doesn't say, "Alleluia, let's go see him." He says, "Really? Can anything good come out of Nazareth?" Can the hope and desperation that I carry within me find an answer and a fulfillment in the real world, this drab, wearisome world where nothing new and truly good ever happens?

When Jesus meets Nathanael, he does not rebuke him for lack of faith or for his skepticism or for dissing Jesus's hometown. Instead, he praises him for being without guile, for being honest and open about both his hope and his hopelessness, his desperation and his despair. And Jesus tells Nathanael that he knows and sees him in all the transparency of his guilelessness. And when Nathanael realizes that Jesus knows him and sees him in the very depths of his being, with all the light and darkness there, he recognizes that his hope has been realized and that his despair was ungrounded: "Rabbi, you are the Son of God! You are the King of Israel!"

My brothers and sisters, this is the kind of guilelessness that we are called to practice during this season of Great Lent. Throughout the season of Great Lent, the church proclaims to us that Christ is risen from the dead. The church says to us: We have found the one who has conquered sin and death and made all things new. Throughout this season of Lent, we are called to get in touch with our desperation for this good news. At the same time, we should also be guileless in confronting our despair and skepticism and bringing them before Jesus in prayer: Can this good news become manifest in the Nazareth of our ordinary daily lives? Can the new heaven and new earth really appear in South Bend, at our little Byzantine Catholic community of Notre Dame? Can the Nazareth of this little community in this chapel really be the place where the risen Christ appears?

My brothers and sisters, "Christ is risen!" is not some deceitful slogan; it's not some beguiling pep chant. It's meant to be true and real and it says to us that everything has been renewed in Christ. And throughout this Lent, we are called to receive this newness, to renew the image of God within us, to receive the image of the risen Christ, to become self-iconographers, through the grace of Christ, of our own resurrection.

Let us respond to this call with authenticity and guilelessness, as we approach the holy table and partake of the life and saving death of the risen Lord, who says to each one of us, "Follow me. Let us walk together, in transparency and guilelessness, through the way of the cross, to the glory of my resurrection." To him be eternal glory and praise, and to the Father and the Holy Spirit, now and forever. Amen.

Guilelessness and Being Beguiled by God

Hebrews 11:24–26, 32–40; 12:1–2; John 1:43–51

Brothers and sisters who are dearly beloved in Christ Jesus our Lord:

As we complete today the first week of the holy season of Lent, I think we are all in a state of shock and pained bewilderment at the atrocities going on in Ukraine.* The constant display of these atrocities before the eyes of all the world, thanks to intense media coverage, should also remind us of other atrocities that have been going on for some time now but in which we seem to have lost interest—in places like Yemen and Syria, for example, and also Afghanistan, in which active conflict has now given way to mass starvation.

In the face of all this display of evil, it is understandable if we feel that it is hard to concentrate on the simple and quiet practices of Lent. We may also be finding it diffi-

* This sermon was preached on March 6, 2022, shortly after the Russian invasion of Ukraine.

cult to have a lively hope that our Lenten observances will really lead to a transformation of our lives and the life of the world. What good will our little Lenten observances do in the face of the evil that runs amok and seems to reign over all the world?

On the face of it, today's gospel does not seem to offer much help in answering this question. Even apart from the distress of our current circumstances, it seems like a strange gospel to read for the first Sunday of Lent, which is also the Sunday in which we celebrate the veneration of icons. Why this gospel, in particular, for the first Sunday of Lent?

The conversation between our Lord and Nathanael, which is the main content of today's gospel, is also strange in itself. In a few short lines of conversation, Nathanael goes through a complete transformation, from being seemingly snobbish and dismissive and skeptical of good news—"Can anything good come out of Nazareth?"—to being an enthusiastic follower and admirer of Jesus: "Rabbi, you are the Son of God! You are the King of Israel." All the explanation that we are given for this sudden and complete transformation is that Jesus told Nathanael that he saw him under the fig tree. Even if Jesus showed Nathanael that he had powers to see things from afar, is that really enough to make him the Son of God and the King of Israel?

Given the strangeness of this story, some people have tried to explain it by speculating that Nathanael must have had some momentous experience under the fig tree—maybe a vision of the coming Messiah—and so he associated Jesus with the content of this vision. But I think that we are on safer ground just going with what the Scriptures actually tell us and, I believe that on that basis, it will be revealed to us what the Spirit is saying to us now, through this gospel, in the opening stages of our Lenten journey.

I think that an important clue to the logic of Nathanael's transformation is the combination of his initial skepticism and Jesus's description of him as someone without deceit—or "without guile" in our translation. Nathanael is a skeptical person and he is without guile. That is a distinct personality type. There is a type of person who is skeptical precisely because they can see through deceit; because of their skepticism, they are not easily fooled. Now some people are skeptical and not easily fooled but they try to fool others; they are not easily deceived but they are deceitful. But there are also people who are skeptical and not easily fooled, and they don't try to fool anyone else either. They try not to be either the victims or the perpetrators of deceit. It seems to me that Nathanael was this kind of person. He was a skeptical person; he wasn't going to be taken in by some scam of someone showing up at his door—or under his favorite fig tree—and saying, "We have found the Messiah." He's suspicious that this claim is a deceit, a scam. And he doesn't like scams; he doesn't like to be deceived and he doesn't like to deceive others. And for that, our Lord commends him: "Here is truly an Israelite in whom there is no deceit."

Perhaps you know someone like Nathanael. Or, maybe you recognize yourself as someone like Nathanael. In any case, most of us at least try to be like Nathanael inasmuch as we try to avoid being either deceived or deceitful. And if you're concerned about being deceived, you need to develop a certain habit of skepticism. You need to be on the lookout for scams so that you don't get taken in by them. And that's a good and healthy part of being a functional and mature person, especially if it's combined with the determination not to be deceitful to others.

There is a problem, though, with this kind of clear-eyed sober skepticism and aversion to deceit. Yes, this attitude can protect us against scams in a world that is full of scams, but it can also close us off from the wonderful and mighty works of God, which are not scams but which cannot be accounted for by just common-sense calculations. The problem with being without guile is that it makes it difficult to be beguiled and enchanted, even by God. The problem with fortifying oneself against every kind of deceit is that it can cut off the possibility of having the kind of encounter with God of which the prophet Jeremiah speaks when he cries out to the Lord, "O Lord, you have deceived me and I was deceived; you are stronger than I and you have prevailed." *Jer. 20:7–8*

So, what's the solution, then? In order to allow ourselves to be beguiled by God, do we have to be gullible? In order to allow ourselves to be seduced by God, do we have to be open to seduction and deceit in general?

No. Nathanael shows us the way. He was a skeptical person and a person without guile, neither easily deceived nor deceitful, but he ended up being beguiled by God and seduced and enticed by the Lord, who proved stronger than his skepticism and prevailed over his common sense. How did this happen?

All this happened to Nathanael through the discovery of how much and how deeply he is known by the Lord. Nathanael's wall of skepticism was not broken down because Jesus proved that he can see things from very far away. This wall was broken down when he became convinced that Jesus saw right through him, saw him through and through to the very depths of his being, that Jesus knew him fully at that very moment, just as he was right then and there. He was impressed and overwhelmed and beguiled when Jesus said, "I saw you under the fig tree," not because of Jesus's miraculous eyesight—and I don't think we need to speculate about a vision that he had under the fig tree, about which the Scriptures say nothing at all. Rather, "I saw you under the fig tree," means "I saw you right now, just before you met me. I see you now and I know you fully, as you are, right here and now."

It was then that Nathanael must have had the same kind of experience of which the psalmist sings:

> O Lord, you have searched me and known me.
> You know when I sit down and when I
>   rise up. . . .
> You search out my path and my lying down,
> and are acquainted with all my ways. . . .
> Such knowledge is too wonderful for me;
> it is so high that I cannot attain it.

Ps. 139:1–6

It is because he had that experience that Nathanael cried out in wonderment, "Where do you know me from?" And the only reasonable answer he could come up with was, "You are the Son of God; you are the King of Israel."

So, my brothers and sisters, now we can discover perhaps what the Spirit is trying to tell us through this gospel as we are embarking on our Lenten journey on this first Sunday of Lent. This year, we begin our Lenten journey in circumstances that impel us to be very skeptical about any claims that this world and the powers of this world make about what is true and what is good and what is just. It is good for us to have this kind of skepticism. It is good for us to be on the lookout for the scams of this deceitful world and all its sham powers and dominions. As we begin our Lenten journey, let us, like Nathanael, be without guile, neither deceived nor deceiving, so that the Lord can say of each one of us, "Behold, an Israelite in whom there is no deceit."

But at the same time, let us be aware of the limits of our skepticism. Let us be vigilant in identifying that voice inside us that says, "Can anything good come out of this Lent? Can Jesus really be the Messiah, the Son of God, the King of kings and Lord of lords, if the world is in such an evil mess? Is it not evil tyrants who rule the world and not the Prince of Peace?"

In the face of this secret skepticism—or maybe it's not so secret—we have to remember that Lent is the time for us to be beguiled by God, to be enticed and seduced by the only true God who loves us into being and will love us into eternal glory. And this can only happen when we let God show us how much he knows us as we are right now—under whatever fig tree we may be lying. He knows what is happening in Ukraine and Yemen and Syria and everywhere else. He knows the battle between good and evil that is going on in each of our hearts. He knows how to transform us from our current weak and sinful condition to the image of his risen glory, through the power of his cross.

All this can only be revealed to us through deep and authentic prayer, prayer in which we don't just recite words but really spend good and quality time in intimate communion with the Lord, letting him reveal to us how much he knows us—which is so much more than we know ourselves—and letting him guide us into the knowledge of his victory over death and sin and how we are called to participate in that victory through our Lenten observances.

Only if we do this will we be able to look upon this suffering world, in which evil seems to reign unchecked, and yet be able to see the deeper truth that has been revealed to us that "the kingdom of this world has already become the kingdom of our Lord and his Messiah." Only then will we be able to sing with all those who worship

Rev. 11:15

before the throne of the Lamb, "We give you thanks, Lord
God Almighty, who are and who were, for you have taken
Rev. 11:17 your great power and have begun to reign." He has already
Ps. 110:2 begun to reign even in the midst of his foes, through
the saving power of his death and resurrection. He has
already begun to reign through us and he will reveal to
us—throughout this Lent, if we let him—how we can be
the heralds of the victory of his resurrection.

As we approach the holy table and partake of the feast
of his resurrection that he has prepared for us through the
sacrifice of his body and blood, let us pray, in the power of
the Spirit, that our Lenten observances may advance the
full manifestation of the reign of our Lord and Messiah,
to the glory of God the Father. Amen.

FEAST OF THE ANNUNCIATION

Mary, Our Guide to a Lent "Full of Grace"

Hebrews 2:11–18; Luke 1:24–38

Brothers and sisters who are dearly beloved in Christ Jesus our Lord:

On the surface of things, it seems like only a coincidence, without any particular significance, whenever the Feast of the Annunciation occurs during Lent, as happens very often. Lent is calculated according to the lunar calendar, in relation to the date of Easter, while the Feast of the Annunciation always takes place on March 25, nine months before the celebration of the birth of Christ on December 25. It just happens to be the case that, very frequently, the intersection of these separate calculations results in the occurrence of the Feast of the Annunciation during Lent.

Speaking for myself, I tend to be caught off guard by the occurrence of this feast during Lent. It is hard to know how to be attentive to it in a way that is integrated with the journey of Lent and its orientation to Easter. At best, it seems like a bit of a break, an unanticipated oasis in the middle of our journey through the seeming desert of our Lenten observances.

And yet, it would be strange if God's providential wisdom, which arranges all things well, intends to convey to us no meaning at all through this seeming coincidence. Indeed, perhaps the very fact that this feast tends to take us by surprise, like an unanticipated gift, while we are focused on the efforts of our Lenten observances, is precisely the key to how it fits into our Lenten journey.

Wis. 8:1

Our Lenten observances, if we take them seriously, take work. If we experience no effort, no exertion in our Lenten practices, then we are not taking this holy season seriously. And yet, there is always the danger that we can perceive the work of our Lenten observances as a laborious effort to earn our salvation instead of as a participation in the gifts that God has graciously given us. If this perception secretly creeps into our Lenten observances, it can lead to both resentment and discouragement. We can end up resenting God for demanding that we do extra work during Lent in order to earn a ticket to the celebration of Easter. Or, we can be discouraged because we cannot imagine the quantity or level of prayer or fasting or almsgiving that can earn our participation in the new life that flows out of our Lord's resurrection.

But, of course, the truth is that our Lenten observances are not intended to earn our salvation. Rather, they are the means by which we take ownership of the gift and grace of our participation in the risen life of Christ. During Lent, we do real spiritual work, but all this work is a work of grace.

To see our Lenten observances as the work of grace—indeed to see all the work of our Christian discipleship as the work of grace—we can do no better than to look to Mary, the one who above every other creature is "full

of grace." On the Feast of the Annunciation, it is most *Luke 1:28*
fitting to celebrate Mary as our Lady of Grace, since she
became the Mother of God, not through the normal work
of human procreation and not through any works of the
law by which she earned that unsurpassable blessing,
but only because she believed in the grace and power
of God that was announced and promised to her by the
angel Gabriel.

Let us recall how St. Paul, the apostle of grace, commends to our attention the example of Abraham, who was
promised that his seed will be more numerous than the
stars in the heavens and the sand on the earth and that all
the nations will be blessed in him. Abraham, St. Paul reminds us, believed in God's promise and it was "reckoned
to him as righteousness." But how much more is that righ-   *Gen. 15:6*
teousness that comes by grace to be ascribed to the one   *Rom. 4:22*
who believed in the much greater promise that she will   *Gal. 3:6*
give birth to the eternal seed of the Father, his only begotten Son, the Creator of heaven and earth. Because she
believed in so great a promise, she was granted the grace
of containing the uncontainable God. It is through her,
the one whom every generation since the Annunciation
by the angel has called blessed, that the promise granted
to Abraham is fulfilled, that all the nations will be blessed
in him. We, along with every generation since that blessed   *Gen. 12:3*
announcement, call her blessed and recognize her as the
house of God and the stairway to heaven.   *Gen. 28:12*

St. Paul also wants us to consider the example of Isaac,
the child of the promise, who represents the new covenant
based not on the observance of the law but on the fulfillment of God's gratuitous promise and gracious mercy.   *Gal. 4:21–28*
But if Isaac is the child of promise, Mary is the Mother of
Promise, the one who gave birth to the fulfillment of every
one of God's promises. Celebrating this fulfillment of all

of God's promises in her, she herself proclaimed: "He has helped his servant, Israel, in remembrance of his mercy, according to the promise he made to our ancestors, to *Luke 1:54*   Abraham and to his descendants forever."

And so, my brothers and sisters, in the midst of our Lenten works, as we work out our salvation with fear and trembling, it is most fitting that we consider, through the blessing of this feast in which the grace of our salvation took root in the Virgin's womb, how all this work is really the work of grace. During Lent, we do not subject ourselves to arbitrary hardships as if we are mere slaves, trying to earn a reward from their Master. Rather, through the adoption by grace as God's own sons and daughters, we exert ourselves to fully receive the gifts that God wants to give us, so that we, who are sanctified, and our Lord Jesus Christ, who *Heb. 2:11*   sanctifies us, may have one and the same Father. All our Lenten works are only the means by which God invites us to share in the fruits of the work that the Lord has already performed for us. They are works of grace.

Therefore, we can have full confidence that our Lenten observances of fasting, prayer, and almsgiving are a sure and trustworthy path to salvation if they are performed in the power of God's grace, through the intercession of Our Lady of Grace. We *fast* in order to devote ourselves more wholeheartedly and single-mindedly to the Word of God that has been graciously revealed to us, recognizing that the human being does not live by bread alone but by *Matt. 4:4*   every word that comes from the mouth of God. We *pray* because our souls are impelled to magnify the Lord and we are compelled, in the Spirit, to rejoice in God our Savior, for he has looked with favor and grace on the lowliness *Luke 1:46–48*   of his servants. We *give alms* and share our material goods with the needy, regardless of their merit, because that is the only way to participate in the economy of grace, in which the One who was rich became poor for our sake, in order to share with us the gift of his divinity, not because we merited it, but solely out of the abundance of his loving mercy.   *2 Cor. 8:9*

For all these reasons, my brothers and sisters, we look to Mary, the one who is full of grace, to guide us in carrying out our Lenten observances as truly works of grace, and not just slavish work designed to please and appease our Master. That, I believe, is the special blessing granted to us when we celebrate the Feast of the Annunciation in the midst of Lent. We look to the one who is full of grace to lead us in the way of living a truly graceful, and therefore joyful, Lent.

My brothers and sisters, as we approach the holy table, wisdom calls out to us, as we just read from the book of Proverbs during the Vespers service, "Come, eat of my food, and drink of the wine I have mixed." Through the   *Prov. 9:5* annunciation of the angel to Mary, and her acceptance of that announcement, the eternal Word of the Father mixed his divinity with the flesh and blood that he took from Mary, his mother. Ever since then, the power of his grace has always been and will always be mixed with the blessing of Mary's acceptance and cooperation with this grace. In her company and in communion with all the saints, let us now eat and drink at this banquet of grace, by which all our human work becomes the work of God's grace.

Through the intercession of our Lady of Grace, may the Holy Spirit come upon us and may the Power of the Most High overshadow us through the remaining days of   *Luke 1:35* this holy season, so that we may rejoice and exult in the resurrection of her Son, in everlasting praise of the glory of God our Father, now and forever. Amen.

LENT, PART 2

Last Sunday before
Covid Shutdown

Hebrews 1:10–2:4; Mark 2:1–12

My brothers and sisters who are dearly beloved in Christ Jesus our Lord:

Last Sunday, the first Sunday of Lent, we were offered the grace of communion with our Lord and all the saints through the veneration of icons, the grace of becoming iconographers ourselves by reinscribing the image of God within us, by heeding the voice of Christ who says to each one of us, "Follow me," and by practicing guilelessness and transparency before God through sincere prayer.

This Sunday, as we continue our Lenten pilgrimage toward the glorious feast of the resurrection of Christ,

---

This sermon was preached on March 8, 2020, just as news of the coronavirus was beginning to grow unmistakably ominous. The previous week, students in my classes were still assuring me that "it's not worse than flu." The following week, classes were canceled and the World Health Organization declared a pandemic. The rest is sorrowful history. The homily plays on the trope of a vaccine; at that time a vaccine for Covid-19 had not yet been developed.

we are offered the grace of healing from the paralysis of sin. Today's gospel is timely, not only with respect to our Lenten liturgy but also in relation to the dark cloud that has suddenly overshadowed our world; I mean the threat of the coronavirus. This threat is just another manifestation of the perennial condition of human helplessness, of paralysis, in the face of destructive forces. It is not, at this point at least, by any means the most acute manifestation of this helplessness and paralysis. At this point, the death toll from human violence, from other diseases, and even from suicide is much larger than that of the coronavirus. But it has gotten our attention.

I think that a large part of the reason that we find this corona threat so scary is precisely because it attacks first of all our sense of existential confidence, our delusion that we are masters of our lives. Here is this tiny little microbe running amuck, threatening not only to damage and destroy individual lives, but to wreak havoc with the social fabric of human existence, making the very act of social communion something possibly lethal and deadly. In the face of this threat, we feel helpless, humiliated, and paralyzed.

In today's gospel, our Lord Jesus is telling us that helplessness and paralysis is part of the very nature of sin. I am not saying that the coronavirus is itself caused by sin but rather that the paralysis we feel in trying to respond to it partakes of the general paralysis of the human condition that is induced by sin. Sin disables our spiritual vitality and mobility and paralyzes us at the very core of our being. As soon as we commit sin, we become victims of this paralysis. Even if we are not conscious of committing sin, sin still attacks us and paralyzes us. Just like a deadly virus, sin permeates our broken and spiritually unsanitary world, and it infects every single member of the human race. And the mortality rate of the contagion of sin is 100 percent.

While we wait and pray for a vaccine for this virus, we can be all the more thankful to our merciful God that there is in fact a safe and reliable vaccine for sin. This vaccine is the death and resurrection of the incarnate Word of God, our Lord Jesus Christ. As you know, a vaccine for a disease contains the same germ as the disease itself, but in a weakened, non-lethal, and lifeless form. Through his death, Jesus allowed himself to be infected with the virus of sin; he allowed himself to become a victim of sin and in this way became sin for us, though he himself did not commit sin. He died for us and with us, setting aside his divine immunity. And through his resurrection, he rendered the deadly virus of sin weak and lifeless for all those who have a share in his life-giving death.   2 *Cor.* 5:21

As with other vaccines, some people reject this vaccine and think that the vaccine itself is dangerous and causes disease. Some people think that they do not need the vaccine because they are strong enough to fight all the germs in the world on their own, or because they hope they are lucky enough that they won't run into any of them. But today's gospel reminds us that we are not strong enough to overcome sin on our own; in fact, we are completely helpless and paralyzed in the face of sin and we can only regain our vitality and spiritual mobility by the vaccine of life in Christ.

While today's gospel reveals to us an aspect of the true nature of sin, on the one hand—that sin is paralyzing—it also reveals to us an important aspect of the true nature of faith, the faith that enables us to benefit from the vaccine of redemption in Christ. In the gospel today, we are not told anything directly about the faith of the paralyzed man to whom Jesus granted forgiveness and healing from his paralysis. Rather, we are told about four people who carried him on a stretcher. Because the crowd prevented

them from getting this paralyzed man to Jesus, they went up on the roof and removed the roof and lowered the stretcher down to Jesus, "and seeing their faith, Jesus said
Mark 2:5   to the paralytic, 'Child, your sins are forgiven you.'"

This is very odd, isn't it, that Jesus sees *their* faith, and on the basis of *their* faith, forgives the paralytic and heals him. Why should their faith have anything to do with the forgiveness of the paralytic? But just as Jesus is teaching us in this gospel about the true nature of the disease of sin, as a kind of paralysis, he is also revealing to us the true nature of spiritual health. Jesus is showing us that true spiritual health is a faith that trusts in Jesus not just for the sake of myself but also for the sake of others. True faith is operative only in the form of a communion of love.

The paralyzed man manifested this faith that takes the form of a communion of love by letting himself be carried by the others, and they manifested their faith that works through love by carrying him to Jesus so that he can be healed. And seeing this faith manifested in the communion of love, Jesus granted the man forgiveness and healing.

Jesus did this in keeping with the law of love that the apostle Paul proclaims when he says to us, "Bear one an-
Gal. 6:2   other's burdens and so fulfill the law of Christ." Those who carried the paralyzed man to Jesus fulfilled the law of Christ by bearing the burden of their brother and presenting that burden to Jesus. Christ fulfilled his own law when he granted the wish of this group of men who were carrying the burden of their fellow man and when he granted the wish of the paralyzed man who allowed himself to be carried by his fellow men.

My brothers and sisters, as we are about to embark on the third week of our Lenten journey, let us be attentive to the powerful and transformative wisdom that today's gos-

pel offers us. It teaches us to recognize the deadly threat
of the paralysis of sin. It urges us to seek the vaccine of
participation in the life and death and resurrection of our
Lord Jesus Christ. It shows us that the way of healing faith
is the way of the communion of love.

In today's gospel, Jesus uses a term of tender affection
when he speaks to the paralyzed man; he calls him "child,"
not literally "son." In this liturgy, our Lord also wants to
speak to us with tender affection, an affection of compassion for the paralysis of our sin and for our fears and
everything else that troubles us—whether it's about the
coronavirus or anything else. He invites us to the medicine of his body and blood, which contains the vaccine
that heals all our diseases, and he says to us, "Children, it's
time for your booster shot." Let us come forward, then,
without fear of judgment or condemnation, letting ourselves be carried before him by all the saints and carrying
in our hearts all those in need of our intercession—in fact
carrying in our hearts all the members of our human race,
all of whom are equally in need of his great mercy. Seeing
our faith, may he grant forgiveness and healing and the
full manifestation of his kingdom to this suffering world,
so that every knee may bow and every tongue confess that   *Phil. 2:10–11*
he is the only true loving and saving God, to whom be all
glory and honor, and to his eternal Father and to their
holy and life-giving Spirit, now and always and forever
and ever. Amen.

Drinking from the Cup
of Christ

Hebrews 9:11–14; Mark 10:32–45

Brothers and sisters who are dearly beloved in Christ Jesus our Lord:

Today is the last Sunday of Lent. Next Sunday will be Palm Sunday and we will enter Jerusalem in the Spirit, with the Lord, and will begin our commemoration of his holy passion, his life-giving death, and his glorious resurrection.

Today, this same Lord is sacramentally present in our midst, at this liturgy, and he is leading us and walking ahead of us to Jerusalem. Everything that took place in the gospel that we just read is taking place now, at this liturgy, in the Spirit. The Lord, who is already risen, is walking ahead of us and leading us into a renewed participation in the mystery of his death and resurrection, leading us through the power of the mystery of what happened in the earthly Jerusalem many years ago into the fullness of the reality of the new Jerusalem, where we will live and rejoice for all eternity.

As he is leading us, we also, like the disciples, are *Mark 10:32* "amazed and afraid." We are amazed, as we will be amazed

114

for all eternity, at the unfathomable mystery that God became human and shed his human blood for the salvation of the world and has conquered death and granted us the fullness of eternal life.

But we are also afraid when we think of what is in store for us, personally, as we follow this divine man to his death and we cannot help but wonder what this following will cost us, and whether we will be able to bear the burden of the cross that we have to carry as we follow him.

As we follow him, we entrust this fear to his compassion. At this very liturgy, of which he is the true celebrant, since he is the High Priest who presides at every liturgy, he is leading us with an outpouring of compassion for our weaknesses: "For we do not have a High Priest who is unable to sympathize with our weaknesses, but we have one who in every way has been tested, as we are, yet without sin." As he leads us in the fullness of his compassion, he is attentive to all our anxieties and fears. He is ready to hear all our requests and to give ear to all our pleas.

Heb. 4:15

Perhaps we have no anxieties and fears or requests and pleas to share with him. Perhaps we are just busy going about our lives, buying and selling, studying and teaching, just putting in the obligatory time for going to church and going through our other observances, without real emotional investment, without offering to the Lord a true accompaniment of the heart. In that case, the Lord's lament would sadly apply to us: "they honor me with their lips but their hearts are far from me." In that case, we must cry out to the Lord with all our hearts and say, "Lord, let not our heart be far from you as we follow you on the way of your passion, as we follow you to Jerusalem."

Matt. 15:8

But perhaps we have a request for the Lord that is similar to the request made by James and John in our gospel today, when they came forward to the Lord and said to him, "Teacher, we want you to do for us whatever we ask

Mark 10:35   of you." Before we allow ourselves to feel too superior to
James and John, let us consider that at least they came
forward to the Lord and made their request known to him
and shared the desires of their hearts with the One who
is the fulfillment of every desire. Let us pray for a greater
share in that grace before we disdain these disciples and
look down on them.

We just heard what the request was that they made to
the Lord: "Grant us to sit, one at your right hand and one

Mark 10:37   at your left, in your glory." Again, let us admire these disciples of the Lord before we focus on their shortcomings.
They were looking forward to the glory of the Lord; they
had a sure and confident faith that he will come into his
glory; and they wanted to be close to him in his glory. They
were already envisioning and making plans for life with the
glorified Lord. Perhaps none of these things is really true
for us; probably, all these things are not sufficiently true
for us. So, let us cry out with all our hearts as we follow the
Lord to Jerusalem: "Lord, let us look forward, with a full
and confident faith, to the vision of your glory. And let us
be near you when you come into your glory."

Now, the Lord certainly did not reject their plea to
be close to him in his glory, though he gently reminded
them that the concern for rank is foreign to that glory. But
what he was teaching them, above all, is that the only way
to share in his glory is to drink from the cup that he will
drink from and to be baptized with the baptism that he
will be baptized with.

What is this cup and this baptism?

It is his sacrificial death, which was the fulfillment
of his sacrificial life, his life and death together making
a perfect sacrifice whose glory became fully manifest in
his resurrection. Our epistle reading speaks of this sacri-

fice when it tells us that through the Holy Spirit, Christ "offered himself unblemished to God, thus obtaining for us eternal redemption." Through this complete and *Heb. 9:12* perfect offering of himself to God, in his life and in his death, Christ entered through the greater and perfect tent into the majesty of the divine glory. "This is the cup from *Heb. 9:11* which you must drink, this is the sacrifice which you must offer," says the Lord, "if you want to enter with me into the fullness of glory."

As the High Priest who is the true presider at this liturgy, as he is leading us in the Spirit toward Jerusalem, Christ is inviting each of us today to drink from this cup and to be baptized with the baptism with which he was baptized. He is saying to each one of us, to you and to me: "Are you able to drink the cup that I drink and be baptized with the baptism that I am baptized with?"

But, if you are not only amazed by the mystery of the Lord's drinking that cup for your salvation, but also afraid of the invitation to share in the Lord's cup, remember again his compassion, how he himself was tested in every way, just as we are, though without sin. Remember also *Heb. 4:15* that the Lord himself struggled with drinking that very cup, though he did not waver in his resolve to drink it. When he was being arrested and Peter tried to defend him, he said, "Shall I not drink the cup that the Father has given me?" But still he struggled in the drinking of the *John 18:11* cup, even if he did not waver in his resolve to drink it.

When he was praying in the garden of Gethsemane, at the eve of his passion, he looked deeply into the cup that he was about to drink. What he saw when he looked into that cup was all the evil that has ever been unleashed on all the world: all the sins, the horrors, the cruelty, the torture, the lovelessness, the faithlessness, the hopelessness of all the world, since the first human beings were banished from paradise and since Cain murdered his brother, Abel, down to the last dying breath of the last human being. All this evil was in the cup that he was about to drink. And when he saw all this in the cup that he was about to drink, he was about to die of grief at the very thought of drinking this cup, before he actually drank it. "He was deeply grieved even to death," the Scriptures tells us, "and he threw himself to the ground and prayed, 'Father, if it is

Matt. 26:39   possible, let this cup pass from me.'"

When our Lord considered *what* was in the cup, every fiber of his being resisted the thought of drinking from that cup: "For what fellowship is there between light and

2 Cor. 6:14   darkness, between good and evil?" And how could the
Heb. 1:3   perfect Radiance of the Father's eternal Light relish the prospect of fellowship with all the darkness and sin of all the world? But when our Lord considered *who* was giving him the cup, every fiber of his being embraced the will of the Father and he completed and consummated his sacrificial self-offering to the Father: "My Father, if this cannot

Matt. 26:42   pass until I drink it, your will be done."

By drinking this cup, our Lord consumed and destroyed all the sin of the world in the sacrificial fire of his holiness. He made a purification for all sin, as we read in the Epistle to the Hebrews, and now sits at the right

Heb. 1:3   hand of the Majesty on high. And while sitting at the right hand of the Majesty on High, he has made provision for all the world to be saved through drinking from the same cup that he drank from, the cup in which all the sins of the world are purified, the cup from which everyone who drinks is sanctified and glorified.

My brothers and sisters, each one of us who has been baptized into Christ has been granted a share in the baptism with which he was baptized. Each one of us to whom the Lord calls out—as we will hear him shortly call out to us at this very liturgy, "Drink from this cup, all of you"—has been granted a share in his saving cup. As to what exactly is and will be in this cup, as far as the specific trials and tribulations that will come to us as we carry our crosses, only the Lord knows. It will not be all the evil in the world, as there was in the Lord's cup, but there surely will be evil that we must contend with in our lives. It will not be all the suffering in the world, as there was in the Lord's cup, but there will be suffering, even to the inevitable point of death. Our drinking from this cup will not be the cause of the purification of all the sins of the world, as the Lord's cup was, but it will be a true and effective and glorious participation in the Lord's purification of sin and his final victory over sin and death.

As we approach the holy table, it is the Lord himself who says to each one of us, "Are you able to drink the cup that I drink?" In a few moments, we will carry this cup in procession around the church, and then it will be placed at the holy altar, in preparation for you to drink from it. Let us pray that we will drink from this cup, not only with our mouths but with the fullness of our hearts. May the drinking of this cup, through the grace of the Lord's death and resurrection, enable us through the Spirit to offer ourselves without blemish to God our Father, and may it purify us from every dead work and every sin, that we may *Heb. 9.14* perfectly worship the only true living God, the Father, the Son, and the Holy Spirit, now and forever. Amen.

PALM SUNDAY

The Human Judgment
of God

Philippians 4:4–9; John 12:1–18

My brothers and sisters who are dearly beloved in Christ
Jesus our Lord:

Today, we begin our celebration of Holy Week by
commemorating the entrance of our Lord Jesus into Jerusalem. It is for us a day of great rejoicing, and yet also a
day of judgment.

It is, first and foremost, a day of great rejoicing. Today,
Jesus enters Jerusalem and manifests himself as the true
King of Israel, the Shepherd who lays down his life for
the sheep, the Temple that is not built by human hands *Heb. 9:11*
and that cannot be destroyed by human hands. Today,
Jerusalem, the city of peace, welcomes the King of Peace, *John 2:19*
humble and meek, riding not on a stallion but on a donkey. The Lord of Israel has come to be crowned King of a
kingdom that contains a new heaven and a new earth. His
entrance into Jerusalem brings about a spontaneous jubilation. A new kind of joy has come about, which renews
not only Jerusalem but all the world, of which the prophet

Isaiah had spoken: "Shine, shine, O new Jerusalem, for the
Isa. 60:1   glory of the Lord has shone upon you."

The Lord's entrance into Jerusalem is the historical
foundation for his sacramental entrance into our hearts
and his enthronement in our souls and bodies through
baptism. So, it is fitting that especially today, we heed the
apostle's exhortation: "Rejoice in the Lord always, and
Phil. 4:4   again, I say rejoice." The reason we rejoice is that "the Lord
Phil. 4:5   is near," as the apostle tells us, in a way that could never
have been imagined before the coming of Jesus. He has
set up his kingdom within us, and has mingled his divinity
with our humanity, and given us the opportunity to be
seated with him at the right hand of the Father even in
Eph. 2:6   the midst of this mortal life. So we too, like the children of
Jerusalem, run toward him in spirit and cry out, just as we
just did in the procession, "Hosanna to the Son of David!
John 12:13   Blessed is he who comes in the name of the Lord!"*

At the same time, we have to recognize that today is
a day of judgment, and indeed, of a terrible and fearful
judgment. Why do I say that? Is it because today we will
be judged by Christ and he will separate the sheep from
Matt. 25:31–32   the goats? No, this is not the day for that kind of judgment, which awaits us at the end of time. Today is a day
for another kind of judgment, which is no less terrible and
fearful, maybe even more so. Now, what can be even more
terrible and fearful than standing before the judgment seat
of Christ? Well, the one thing even more terrible and fearful than standing before the judgment seat of Christ is
sitting in judgment over Christ himself.

Yet our judgment of Christ is an indispensable part of
the mystery that we celebrate today. Jesus entered Jerusa-

---

* For the liturgy of Palm Sunday, there is a procession with palms
before the liturgy, in the course of which this verse is repeated.

lem not only to declare the joy of the Lord's return to his temple, not only to manifest himself as the new King of the new Israel, but also to subject his kingship to the judgment of human sinners. Such is the amazing graciousness, and fearful humility, and awesome meekness of God that before he judges us, he submits, and indeed demands, to be judged by us.

And so it happened, that when Jesus entered Jerusalem, he was judged by each person at that time, as each saw fit. A lot of people were happy at first to join the jubilation and to acclaim him king, holding up palm branches and crying out, "Hosanna to the Son of David!" as we did in the procession. But then Jesus started teaching and reprimanding the people for their infidelity and their lack of responsiveness to God's gracious love. He made enemies. And when his enemies confronted him, he did not act like a strong and victorious king. He did not vanquish his enemies and slay them with the breath of his mouth; *2 Thess. 2:8* he did not call down legions of angels to rescue himself from their clutches. We know how people can be mesmer- *Matt. 26:53* ized and won over by those who assert their leadership by claiming to be "winners." But after Jesus entered Jerusalem in triumph, he did not prove to be a winner. He proved to be a loser. He was arrested and put to trial, and his disciples deserted him and fled, and the chief among them said, "I do not know the man." He was put on trial and *Matt. 26:72* subjected to judgment and the verdict was, "He deserves death." And at the hour of his death, many of those who *Matt. 26:66* were yelling out, "Hosanna to the Son of David!" when he entered Jerusalem just a few days before, were now yelling out, "Crucify him, crucify him!" *Matt. 27:22–23*

My brothers and sisters, just as the grace of this feast sacramentally renews the kingship of Christ in us, it also renews the trial of Christ before the judgment seat of the heart of each one of us. We cannot escape this fearful judgment, if we want to keep this feast. Every year, the way to an authentic participation in the mystery of Christ's death and resurrection must pass through this awful burden we must bear of sitting in judgment over the Lord of heaven and earth. Not to enter into this time of judgment is effectively to judge against him, to dethrone him and impeach his lordship.

The Gospels suggest to us a clear path for taking on this judgment in the days ahead, as we make our way to the Holy Triduum. First of all, we should recall the triumphant entry of Christ into our lives, the jubilation that we felt at moments of conversion, when we spontaneously acclaimed him as Lord and King of our hearts and minds. We should also bring to mind the transports of delight that we have experienced when we were moved by the Spirit to pour out our love to him, as Mary did when she *John 12:1–8* anointed his feet with perfume. But we should also recognize all the disappointment and fears and insecurities in our lives, which tempt us to disown Christ and to say, at least with our actions if not with our words, "I do not *Matt. 26:72* know the man." We must admit frankly that even the risen Lord still acts very much like a loser and not a winner, because his kingship, like his entry into Jerusalem, is one of meekness and humility and because, until his second and glorious coming again, the risen Christ still reigns through the cross. His glory is still manifested in us through suffering. Finally, we must take stock of our recurring sins, which cry out, despite our best intentions, "Crucify him, *Luke 23:21* crucify him!"

And after carefully considering all these things, we must render judgment: Is this man truly the Lord of *Gal. 2:20* heaven and earth, "who loved me and gave his life for me" and gave his divine life to me, who deserves the total dedication of my whole being to his service? Or is he just a loser, who deserves, if not death, at least neglect? As I said, not to make this judgment is itself a judgment that, after all, he deserves not much more than neglect.

My brothers and sisters, let us rejoice today, as the apostle encourages us to do, for indeed the Lord is near. But let us also commit ourselves—today and for the rest of this holy week—to enter into the inner chambers of our hearts so that we may render right judgment in the most fearsome trial imaginable, where God himself submits to be judged by us. Let us call on the Holy Spirit, who searches even the deep things of God, to help us render a judgment that is not superficial and facile but issues from the very depths of our being. The eternal Word of the Father, who came into this world not to condemn the world but to save it, now awaits our word of judgment. *1 Cor. 2:10*

John 3:17

As we prepare to deliberate over this awesome judgment that we must make, let us fortify ourselves by partaking of the royal banquet which he has prepared for us by giving us his body and blood for our salvation. Let us taste and see how good is the Righteous One who awaits our just judgment, to whom we also render all glory, honor, and worship, the Father, the Son, and the Holy Spirit, now and forever. Amen. *1 John 2:1*

WHY THE DONKEY?

Philippians 4:4–9; John 12:1–18

Brothers and sisters who are dearly beloved in Christ Jesus our Lord:

Our Lenten journey is now complete. The time to focus on our Lenten disciplines and exertions is over. Now is the time to focus on the grace of the Lord, his exertions on our behalf, his saving passion and life-giving resurrection.

Today, our Lord enters Jerusalem, declaring himself the King of Israel and the King of all the world, our Savior, our Redeemer, the true source of all our joy in this world and the sure guarantor of our eternal joy.

When the Lord enters Jerusalem, the people adorn his path by spreading their cloaks on the road and waving palm branches. They acclaim him as the Messiah by shouting, as we just chanted: "Hosanna to the Son of David! Blessed is he who comes in the name of the Lord! Hosanna in the highest heaven!"

At the same time, our Lord enters Jerusalem accompanied by a great outpouring of the Holy Spirit, which enables the crowd that welcomed Jesus to recognize that his

presence means that "the Lord is near," that it is now time
to "rejoice in the Lord and to rejoice in the Lord always,"   *Phil. 4:4–5*
that "whatever is true, whatever is honorable, whatever is
just, whatever is pure, whatever is pleasing, whatever is
commendable, every excellence and everything worthy
of praise"—is present in all its fullness in this man who   *Phil. 4:8*
is now riding on a donkey, who is also God eternally enthroned in the heavens.

Today, we too, no less than that crowd in Jerusalem,
feel this joy inspired by the Spirit, as we too carry our
palms and chant our praises and rejoice in the Lord who
has come near to save us.

At the same time, we know something that crowd did
not know when they were welcoming Jesus. We know that
all this joy, all this bedlam of festivity, is about to go hor-
ribly wrong. In the Gospel of Matthew, immediately after
Jesus's triumphant and joyful entrance into Jerusalem, he
goes on a vandalism spree. He throws out people from
the temple; he overturns tables and chairs; he tells people
that the kingdom of God will be taken away from them;
and he even messes with the fig trees. Not to be outdone,
the leaders arrange for Jesus to be arrested and flogged
and crucified. At the end, when Pilate says to the people,
"What should I do with Jesus who is called the Messiah?,"   *Matt. 27:22*
they do not say, "Hosanna to the Son of David. Blessed
is he who comes in the name of the Lord." They say: "Let   *Matt. 27:22*
him be crucified."

What went wrong? How did everything go wrong so
quickly, so drastically? I think that the heart of the answer
to this question is that the people became quickly disappointed and embittered and finally hostile when they
realized just how unimpressive, how impotent, and even
ridiculous was this self-proclaimed king. He did, after all,
announce his kingship riding on a donkey. Yes, that was a

Zech. 9:9 fulfillment of prophecy, but it is still ridiculous. This was a self-proclaimed king who seemed to be not only unable but even unwilling to defend himself or his followers. A king who allowed himself to be spat upon and mocked and beaten. And yet, despite all this and despite his apparent humility on his first entrance, he still seemed to at least insinuate exorbitant claims about being God's Son and he still claimed for himself the authority to take over the temple where the God of Israel is supposed to dwell.

It should not take too much power of imagination to recognize the dilemma of the people around Jesus who were trying to make up their mind about him. Is he the glorious Messiah or is he just a ridiculous pretender? If he's so humble, why is he so demanding and even condemning? Why did he bring so much joy at his entrance and then wreak so much havoc immediately afterwards?

My brothers and sisters, the sacramental grace of our great feast today brings us the same joy, the same bedlam of festivity, that swept over and lifted up that crowd in Jerusalem. The same Spirit that inspired that crowd now inspires us to recognize in Jesus the joy of the Lord, the nearness of the Lord, and everything true and honorable and excellent and praiseworthy. But this same Spirit and this same sacramental grace also place before us today the same dilemma faced by that crowd. I think that all of us here today have experienced the nearness of the Lord and the glory and power of the Lord in Jesus, the Messiah, the Christ. But we have also experienced the apparent weakness and impotence and ridiculousness of his kingship, the donkey-ness of his glory.

Why the donkey? Why not just straight plain glory? All of us can find a donkey somewhere in the way Jesus approaches us, a sign of contradiction, a humility and meekness of his lordship that is much less attractive in real life than it is in mere thought. There are so many ways in which Jesus is weak in our lives, and not powerful. There are so many ways in which his presence seems to be so un-glorious. Yet he still claims his kingship. He is still so demanding. He is not ashamed of his weakness but in- sists that this weakness is the real sign of God's strange power that manifests itself precisely through weakness and seeming impotence. What are we to make of all this? *2 Cor. 12:9* It is a dilemma.

But, as I said, to be placed in this dilemma is the very grace offered to us today. We must not evade it. To evade it is to fail to consider it with full seriousness. To just wait till the next liturgy and the next set of beautiful chants is to neglect and despise the grace offered to us today. *1 Tim. 4:14* In order to receive this grace, we must come to a deci- sion: Is Jesus our King, the true and sovereign King of our hearts and minds? Yes or No? And what about the donkey? Where is Jesus's donkey in my life? Can I accept the kingship of Jesus once the donkey is thrown into the bargain? We sing in the kontakion today: "O Christ God, enthroned in Heaven and on earth riding on a donkey." There is the dilemma in a nutshell. Jesus so often, more often than not, appears on earth riding on a donkey. Can we really believe that this same Jesus, riding on a donkey, is enthroned in heaven?

My brothers and sisters, you and I, of ourselves, can have no convincing answer to this question. Only the Spirit of God, the Spirit of Truth who searches the deep things of God, can answer that question for us in a truly *John 16:13* convincing way. All we have to do is allow ourselves to *1 Cor. 2:10* dwell on this question. All we have to do is allow our- selves to be confronted with this dilemma. God's Spirit will do the rest. Let us now implore God our Father to send down his Spirit upon us at this very liturgy, through the sharing in the self-offering of our Lord's body and blood, so that this same Spirit may enable us to truly welcome our divine King who comes to us today riding on a donkey and to say, "with all our whole soul and our whole mind":* Hosanna to the Son of David! Hosanna in the highest heaven! Blessed is he who comes in the name of the Lord! Amen.

* Prayer from the "Ecumenic Litany" after the sermon: "Let us all say with our whole soul and our whole mind, let us all say: Lord, have mercy."

The Joy of Christ

Philippians 4:4–9; John 12:1–18

Brothers and sisters who are dearly beloved in Christ Jesus our Lord:

Today, we sacramentally welcome the Lord, in the Spirit, as he enters Jerusalem, the city of peace, the city of the great King, where the Prince of Peace died on the cross and, through his death and resurrection, became the King and Lord of all the earth, so that at his name every knee should bend, in heaven and on earth and under the earth, and every tongue confess and praise him, saying, "Jesus Christ is Lord; hosanna to the Son of David." *Ps. 48:2*

Phil. 2:10–11
Matt. 21:9

Last Sunday, as we followed our Lord on his way to Jerusalem, we reminded ourselves that everything that took place as reported in the gospel takes place for us now in the liturgy, through the grace of the Spirit. In the feast that we celebrate today, I think it is permissible to say that what is happening now in this liturgy even surpasses what happened then, in the earthly Jerusalem. At that time and place, Jesus's kingship was only proclaimed in advance; it was not yet achieved and consummated. This consummation was brought about only by his death

133

and resurrection. But now, at this liturgy, it is the crucified and risen Lord who enters in our midst and proclaims his lordship through the Holy Spirit that he has poured out on us, and is enthroned on our praises as we sing to him, *Ps. 22:3* "Hosanna to the Son of David; blessed is he who comes *Matt. 21:9* in the name of the Lord."

As much as the Spirit stirred the hearts of that crowd in Jerusalem to rejoice at the entrance of Jesus into the earthly Jerusalem, this same Spirit inspires in us an even greater rejoicing as the Lord enters in our midst today to renew the power of his death and resurrection among us. And the apostle Paul exhorts us to heed this stirring of the Spirit among us today when he says, "Rejoice in the *Phil. 4:4–5* Lord always, and again I say rejoice. The Lord is near."

Yet, perhaps, we are concerned that it might be too soon to rejoice just now. We have not yet arrived, after all, at the celebration of Easter. In the coming days, as we fol- *John 16:6* low the Lord in his passion, our hearts will be full of sorrow and while we might be near the Lord in his suffering, joy might seem very far from us. Even more, it might seem to us that it is even too soon to rejoice as long as we are still pilgrims on this earth, traveling through this vale of tears, where suffering and affliction are always pressing, if not on us personally, certainly on so many of our fellow human beings. Is it not insensitive and even callous to rejoice when there is so much suffering and sadness in the world? Did not our Lord himself say, "Blessed are those who *Matt. 5:4* mourn"? Is not mourning and weeping a more fitting and decent response to the evil and misery of this world? When we see the terrible ravages of senseless war in Ukraine and Syria and other places in the world, to mention just one of the many evils of this world, should we not say with the prophet Jeremiah, "O that my head were a spring of water, and my eyes a fountain of tears, so that I might weep day *Jer. 9:1* and night for the slain of my poor people!"

Yet again, we still have to contend with the words of the apostle that we just read, which are words of inspired Scripture: "Rejoice in the Lord always, again I say rejoice." The apostle does not merely encourage us to rejoice; he commands us, with the full authority bestowed on him by the Holy Spirit to proclaim the gospel of Jesus Christ. In commanding us to rejoice, he is simply being faithful to the gospel preached by our Lord himself, who said to his disciples, "I have said these things to you so that my joy may be in you, and that your joy may be complete." *John 15:11*

So then, are we supposed to mourn or to be joyful? Which one is it?

My brothers and sisters, among the many mysteries of our Christian life, there is the great mystery that it is possible for us, and indeed it is commanded of us, to mourn and to be joyful at the same time. We mourn and weep because of all the suffering and evil in the world, including the suffering we inflict on others and the evil in our own hearts. But we rejoice because the Lord is near, because the Lord has come so near to us in the midst of our suffering and evil as to take all this suffering and evil upon himself, and to transform it into the joy of salvation by the power of his death and resurrection.

Our Lord himself lived out the mystery of joyful suffering and suffering joy throughout his earthly life. He wept at the death of Lazarus but he rejoiced after reviving him from *John 11:35* death and rejoiced again while he had dinner with Lazarus. He also allowed Mary, the sister of Lazarus, to rejoice at his presence and to anoint his feet in preparation for his burial and the fragrance of that joy filled the house. *John 12:3*

Just as Jesus is the "pioneer and perfecter of our faith," *Heb. 12:2* as we read in the book of Hebrews, so he is also the pioneer and perfecter of the mystery of our joyful suffering. That same passage in the book of Hebrews tells us that "for the sake of the joy that was set before him [he] en-

Heb. 12:2   dured the cross." And what was that joy that was set before him, that our Lord set before himself, as he endured the suffering of the cross? It was not the joy of his own personal resurrection and liberation from suffering. If he had

Phil. 2:6   wanted to hold on to that joy and to grasp it for himself, he would never have taken on the suffering of the cross in the first place. No, the joy that Jesus set before himself as he endured suffering for our sake was the joy of *our* salvation, the joy of saving us from suffering and death. This was the joy that sustained Jesus throughout his sufferings.

It was this very joy in which the Lord rejoiced in the salvation he worked for us that fulfilled the words of the prophet Zephaniah when he said:

> Thus says the Lord: Shout for joy, O daughter of Sion! Sing joyfully, O daughter of Jerusalem! Be glad and exult with all your heart! The LORD has removed your iniquities. He has ransomed you from the hand of your
>
> *Zeph. 3:14–17*   enemies. The King of Israel, the LORD is in your midst. . . . The LORD, your God, is in your midst to save you. He will rejoice over you with gladness, and renew you in his love, and he will sing joyfully because of you, as one sings at festivals.

My brothers and sisters, today we are singing joyfully, as one sings at festivals, because the Lord is in our midst; he has come near to us to remove our iniquities, to ransom us from the hand of our enemies; he is in our midst to save us. But if we look into the depths of our own joy, we find that it is the Lord's joy that sustains our joy. It is he who rejoices over us with gladness as he renews us, at this liturgy, in his love. *He* is singing joyfully, at this liturgy, because of us and our salvation, "as one sings at festivals," as only God can sing at the festival of the salvation of his people!

My brothers and sisters, just as the peace of God passes all understanding, so does the joy of the Lord pass all understanding. As long as we are on this earth, the joy of the Lord does not cancel out the suffering that comes from carrying our crosses. As we sing in the Easter liturgy, "it is through the cross that joy has come into all the world." It is through our sharing in the suffering of Christ that all our sufferings can be converted into joy. This process will be perfectly completed only when we are fully assimilated to the resurrection of our Lord and there will be no more suffering left, only perfect joy.

Phil. 4:7

But until that time, of which we will be granted a sacramental participation in a week's time, we can still set before us this joy of resurrection as we endure our sufferings. We can still heed the apostle's exhortation to "rejoice in the Lord always, and again I say rejoice." And if we ask St. Paul whether it is possible for us to keep rejoicing in the midst of our suffering and our mourning over the suffering of the whole world, he will remind us: "We boast in our sufferings, knowing that suffering produces endurance, and endurance produces character, and character produces hope, and hope does not disappoint us because God's love has been poured into our hearts, through the Holy Spirit that has been given us." And if we ask him again for reassurance that our joy in the Lord will not be overcome by the suffering and sadness of the world, he will remind us again that the joy of the Lord is a treasure we carry "in clay jars, so that it may be made clear that this extraordinary power belongs to God and does not come from us. We are afflicted in every way but not crushed; perplexed, but not driven to despair; persecuted, but not forsaken; struck down but not destroyed, always carrying in the body the death of Jesus, so that the life of Jesus may also be made visible in our bodies."

Rom. 5:3–5

2 Cor. 4:7–10

Brothers and sisters, how gracious is the Lord's mercy that before he asks us to accompany him in his passion and before he invites us to unite our sufferings with his sufferings, he comes today to plant his joy in our hearts, the joy that this world can never take away, the joy that conquered death itself.

As we continue our celebration of the Lord's mysteries, the power of the life and death of our Lord is about to be manifested at the holy altar, and with it the power not only to endure our sufferings but even to rejoice and to boast in our suffering. The fullness of the joy of the Lord will be present in his body and blood at this holy altar, the very same joy that he set before him as he endured the cross, the very same joy that he took in accomplishing our salvation, the very same joy with which he sings the song of our salvation for all eternity.

Let us also sing to him our praises as we approach the holy table to partake of this feast of joy, saying, "Hosanna to the Son of David. Blessed is he who comes in the name of the Lord—in the name of the one true God, the Father, the Son, and the Holy Spirit, now and forever." Amen.

GREAT AND HOLY FRIDAY

Loving the Compassion
of Christ

Ezekiel 37:1–14; 1 Corinthians 5:6–8;
Galatians 3:13–14; Matthew 27:62–66

My brothers and sisters dearly beloved in Christ Jesus our
crucified Lord:

It seems to me that at the heart of this glorious liturgy
of the funeral of Christ that we are celebrating this eve-
ning, there is a powerful combination of two themes. On
the one hand, there is the theme of God's compassionate
self-emptying, the contemplation of which draws us into
the unfathomable depths of the mystery of God's love for
humanity. On the other hand, there is the focus on the
very human expressions of affection and care toward the
suffering and dead Jesus, a focus which especially draws
our attention to the figures of Mary, Joseph of Arimathea,
and the myrrh-bearing women. The connection between
these two themes may not be obvious and it is not spelled
out explicitly in the liturgical texts, and yet I think this
connection is central to our experience of the power of
this liturgy.

The theme of God's incomprehensible self-emptying in Christ was already a high point of the service for Holy Thursday, when we chanted:

> Today He who hung the earth upon the waters
>   is hung upon a tree.
> The King of the angels is crowned with thorns.
> He who wraps the heavens in clouds is
>   wrapped in the purple of mockery.
> He who set Adam free receives blows upon
>   His face.
> The Bridegroom of the Church is held up
>   with nails.
> The Son of the Virgin is pierced with a spear.*

We continue this theme throughout tonight's service, when we sing in our lamentations: "How, O life, did you die and abide in a grave?"** and "Christ, my Savior, the sun hid its face and the earth trembled when you, O unwavering Light . . . sank to darkness and the grave."***

The words of these prayers echo what many of the fathers of the church tell us, that God's compassionate self-emptying in Christ shows forth God's glory in an even more powerful and mysterious way than God's act of bringing about and sustaining creation.**** After all, many people throughout the ages have concluded on the basis of reason alone that there must be a creative principle and a first cause, an infinite and necessary being who has brought all finite things into being and who sustains them

---

* Mother Mary and Kallistos Ware, *The Lenten Triodion* (South Canaan, PA: St. Tikhon's Seminary Press, 2002), 313m altered.

** *Lenten Triodion*, 623, altered.

*** *Lenten Triodion*, 612, altered.

**** See Gregory Nyssa, *Catechetical Orations* 24.

in being. But no one, on the basis of reason alone, has ever inferred or guessed or imagined that such a perfect and infinite being would assume the form of a finite being and consent to be hit and spat upon and punched in the face and nailed to a cross and put to death, without invoking any of his divine power in self defense. This mystery has only been revealed to the world through Christ, who has manifested God's weakness as infinitely more powerful than human strength and God's foolishness as infinitely more wise than human wisdom.

1 Cor. 1:25

But alongside this focus on the mystery of God's self-emptying, our services today also shine a spotlight on simple and spontaneous expressions of human affection for Jesus at the time of his suffering and death. We overhear Mary lamenting at the tomb of Jesus: "I alone among women without pain gave birth to you, but now I bear severe pain by your suffering, O my divine Son."* We see Joseph taking down the body of Jesus from the cross and wrapping it in a shroud so that he can be buried with dignity. And we celebrate the myrrh-bearing women who went to the tomb to anoint Jesus and were the first to discover that the tomb was empty. Clearly, today's liturgy wants us to see Mary, Joseph of Arimathea, and the myrrh-bearing women as models of how we should love Jesus in his suffering and death.

But what is the connection between these two themes of the transcendent self-emptying of God, on the one hand, and the human expressions of affection for the suffering and dead Jesus, on the other? On a very simple but very powerful level, we can see that the one is a response to the other: we respond to God's self-emptying love by pouring out our own love for the suffering of Christ. But I

* *Lenten Triodion*, 612, altered.

think that we can go even deeper and say that it is precisely devotion to the suffering Christ that grants us a real participation in the mystery of God's self-emptying.

After all, what do we love when we love the suffering Christ? We do not love the suffering itself that is inflicted on him; we lament this suffering, we do not love it. But then do we love Christ and simply put up with his suffering as just bad stuff that happened to him, the way we can love a friend who is suffering from a terrible disease? No, our love of the suffering Christ is still different from that, because even though we do not love the suffering itself, we do love the fact that he undertook this suffering on our behalf. But if we love Christ for taking on this suffering on our behalf, that means that when we love him in his suffering, we are loving his compassion for us that is manifested in this suffering. And that is how we are led from our devotion to the suffering Christ to the heights and depths of the mystery of God's loving self-emptying on our behalf.

The further we travel within that mystery, the more we will experience what no human tongue can utter and what no human mind can entirely comprehend. And yet our liturgy today evokes some glimpses of this unspeakable mystery. After all, is not our loving lamentation for the suffering and dead Christ a certain participation in God's loving lamentation for the suffering of humanity and our death through sin? Then must we not say that something like our liturgy of lamentation tonight transpired within the heart of the Trinity, when humanity sinned and became estranged from God and brought death on itself?

When we contemplate Joseph's wrapping the dead Jesus with a clean burial shroud, can we not see a glimpse there of the Father's compassion in clothing Adam with the

Gen. 3:21   garments of skin after he had sinned and then ultimately clothing him with the flesh of his only begotten Son?

Is not the impulse that motivated the myrrh-bearing women to anoint the dead body of Jesus in fact a reflection of the love whereby Christ poured himself out as the myrrh that healed our corruption? We just sang after all: "Truly, O Logos, you *are* myrrh most precious which is poured forth. Therefore, unto You, the true living God, the myrrh-bearing women brought most precious myrrh."*

What I am saying might seem outlandish, but in fact it is simply an application of the simple scriptural teaching that we find in the first epistle of the evangelist John, "We love because he first loved us." We love Christ in his suffer- *1 John 4:19* ing because he first loved us in our suffering. His suffering was due to nothing else than his love for us and there is no other way to enter into the mystery of his love for us in our suffering except by loving him in his suffering.

My beloved brothers and sisters, this mystery contains a lesson in Christian discipleship that we urgently need in our own time. Not only outside the church but even within the church, we have found all kinds of pretexts for withholding our affection and even our attention from the suffering of Jesus. All too many Christians now consider it morbid and unbalanced or masochistic or a glorification of suffering itself if we pay too much attention or express too much devotion to the suffering of Christ. The result is that it has become almost a positive spiritual principle in our time to abandon Christ in his suffering!

But our liturgy today leads us in the exact opposite direction. In fact, the immediate directive we get from our liturgical prayers today is that we must devote this very special time between our commemoration of Christ's death and our celebration of his resurrection precisely to loving Christ in his suffering and death, like Mary; and wrapping

* *Lenten Triodion*, 633, altered.

his dead and broken body with our affection, like Joseph of Arimathea; and anointing it with our heartfelt devotion, like the myrrh-bearing women. In fact, only if we *love* Christ through his suffering and death will we be able to experience his resurrection precisely as the final victory of Love itself, rather than merely a miracle of sheer power.

When we love Christ in his suffering and death, we love him from a faith that confesses that he loved us literally to death, and we love him out of a sure hope that he will love us into resurrection.

Let us adore his passion, so that we might share in the victory of his compassion, which is displayed in the glory of his resurrection! Amen.

God's Falling in Love

Ezekiel 37:1–14; 1 Corinthians 5:6–8,
Galatians 3:13–14; Matthew 27:62–66

My brothers and sisters who are dearly beloved in Christ
Jesus our Lord:

We celebrate tonight the mystery of the suffering and
death of the incarnate and eternal Son of God, a mystery
that stupefies our minds and hearts. Our minds cannot
comprehend the greatness of the divine condescension
displayed in the suffering and death of the Lord Jesus, and
our hearts cannot fathom the greatness of the love that
prompted him to perform this incomprehensible deed. So
we celebrate this great mystery of our salvation in a helplessness of perplexity. In the beautiful lamentations we
have just sung, we rejoice in this perplexity as the image
imprinted on our hearts and minds of the transcendence
of the mystery that we celebrate.

But we know that for those who do not share our
faith, and perhaps even for us in our weaker moments, the
events that we celebrate today are not so much incomprehensible as nonsensical. Moreover, they are perceived not
so much as overwhelming our affection, but as repugnant

to our feeling. Why should the suffering of an innocent man bring about our salvation? And how could this innocent suffering man be the eternal God?

Of course, since the beginning of the proclamation of the gospel, the mystery of Christ crucified has been a scandal and a stumbling block for both Jews and Gentiles, and, yes, even for Christians. But, in our own time, what makes this mystery especially alien to us is our contemporary incapacity to comprehend or even acknowledge—even on a merely human level—the value of suffering, and the deep and necessary bonds between suffering and love. We have become so impoverished in our capacity to appreciate the mystery of this bond between suffering and love that we must travel to a different time, a time less deranged than ours, to retrieve a simple intuition of the human level of this mystery, so that we can ascend from there to the inexpressible heights of its divine fulfillment.

1 Cor. 1:23

As a dramatization of the human level of this mystery, we can recall a scene in Shakespeare's play *Othello* in which Othello speaks of how he and his wife, Desdemona, fell in love. In this monologue, he tells of how Desdemona was always eager to listen to stories about his past trials and sufferings: his violent battles, his enslavement by his enemies, and all his other past misfortunes. He says that she would "with a greedy ear devour up my discourse," and afterwards, he says, "she gave me for my pains a world of sighs." He ends his story of how he and Desdemona fell in love by saying, "She loved me for the dangers I had passed and I loved her that she did pity them."*

"She loved me for the dangers I had passed and I loved her that she did pity them." Which is to say: She loved me

---

* *Othello*, act 1, scene 3.

on account of my suffering, and I loved her because she had compassion on my suffering. She loved me in recompense for my suffering and I loved her because she willingly chose to relive my sufferings with me and to enfold my suffering in her love. And because she relived my suffering with me in love, even my sufferings became lovely; they became love-filled; they became the very matter and content of her love.

Now, is this not in fact the true touchstone of authentic love, that the lover should seek to make the suffering of the beloved one's own, that the lover should seek to devour the sufferings of the beloved with "a greedy ear" and a greedy heart, to take in these sufferings and suffuse them with love, and exhale them with a world of love-filled sighs? Is it not most fitting, then, that the beloved should love in return, with a heart full of gratitude, the one who loves with such compassion? Can there be a true and authentic love without two people exchanging and reciprocating these offices of lover and beloved, these offices of rendering compassion and gratitude for compassion rendered?

My brothers and sisters, at the heart of our Christian faith and at the heart of the mystery that we celebrate today is the wondrous claim that this true touchstone of authentic love is also present, in a supereminent way, in God's love for us. All the beautiful lamentations and hymns we have been singing tonight are ultimately saying nothing more or less than precisely this—that, in Christ, God's love was revealed to us as a love that was greedy to devour up the long sad tale of our sufferings. Our loving God, our God who is love, was greedy to love us through *1 John 4:8* all the dangers that we had passed and all the dangers that had overcome us. He was greedy even to be devoured by the death that devoured us, so that his love can accompany us even in our being devoured by death. But when death tried to devour him, the eternal God, it was his eternal and indestructible love that devoured death. So *1 Cor. 15:54* our death was swallowed up in the victory of his love. In exchange for all the suffering he took from us, he gave us for our pains not just a world of sighs, but he sighed forth his own Holy Spirit, the Spirit that binds together his love for his eternal Father and the Father's eternal love for him, saying, "Come from the four winds, O Spirit, O Spirit of eternal and vivifying love, and breathe upon these dead *Ezek. 37:9* bones, that they may come to life."

Now, it can happen with human love, as in the story of Othello and Desdemona, that someone may fall in love with another precisely *because* of their suffering, so that it is co-suffering, compassion, that gives birth to love. That was not the case with God. God did not *fall* in love with us *because* of our sufferings and the dangers we had passed, the dangers that overwhelmed us and brought us to ruin and death. God loved us in Christ even before the *Eph. 1:4* foundation of the world! And yet, what we are celebrating today is precisely the great mystery that God did indeed fall in love with us, in Christ. Before the incarnation of the eternal Beloved Son of the Father, God had not, in fact, *fallen* in love with us. He simply *was* in love with us. But in the fullness of time, this same eternal beloved Son of the Father accomplished God's falling in love with us by descending from the exalted form of God and assuming *Phil. 2:6–8* the form of a fallen servant. In Christ, God fell in love with us by falling not only to the level of our humanity but even to the level of our sinful misery and our death, redeeming us from the curse by devouring this curse in himself *Gal. 3:13* and becoming a curse for us. He did all of this because he "did pity" us, and wanted not only to rescue us from the dangers we had passed but to devour and appropriate to himself all the sufferings and pains that we incurred in our struggles with these dangers and in our defeats and failures, even to the final defeat of death. In doing all this, he cancelled the debt of our infinite offense against his glory and replaced it with the debt of an infinite gratitude for his loving mercy. What joy it will be, my brothers and sisters, to spend our eternity paying back this infinite debt, which we are already paying back, even in this liturgy.

My brothers and sisters, we are sometimes inclined to say in these days between Holy Friday and Easter that the suffering and death of Christ does not have the last word. The last word, we say, belongs to the resurrection. But whatever we might mean by that, it is not, as it stands, completely true. At least, we must also say that the cross of Christ *is* the last word, inasmuch as the suffering love of God, the fallen love of God, will be the subject of our joy for all eternity, as it is already in the beautiful lamentations we have been singing tonight.

After we ourselves are devoured by death, only to devour death through Christ's victorious love; after this whole world is uprooted and folded up like an old piece of cloth; when we come face to face with the Lord and look upon the one whom we have pierced, the one who allowed himself to be pierced by his unfathomable love for us; then, we will forever sing of how this great and glorious God fell in love with us in Christ, and accompanied us through all the dangers we had passed, and how we came to love him with an eternal and undying gratitude, above all because he "did pity" us.

As we continue our adoration of the Lord's passion, in anticipation of the celebration of his glorious resurrec-

Ps. 102:26

1 Cor. 13:12

Zech. 12:10

John 19:37

tion, let us now also anticipate this eternal celestial liturgy, as we proclaim in the Spirit:

Rev. 5:13   "To the one seated on the throne and to the Lamb who was slain be blessing and honor and glory and might forever and ever."

Saved by a Broken Heart

Ezekiel 37:1–14; 1 Corinthians 5:6–8;
Galatians 3:13–14; Matthew 27:62–66

My brothers and sisters who are deeply beloved in our
crucified Lord Jesus Christ:

A disciple of Christ once said, "The heart has its reasons, which reason does not know.... We know the truth
not only by the reason but by the heart."*

Today, both our hearts and our reason are suspended
as if upon a cross of perplexity and bewilderment as we
celebrate unfathomable mysteries at which even the angels are aghast.

We celebrate the mystery of Life itself lying in a grave.

We celebrate the mystery of the Creator of heaven and
earth buried beneath the earth he created.

We celebrate the mystery of the One who neither
slumbers nor sleeps accepting the slumber of death. *Ps. 121:4*

How can our reason—which derives its power and its
light from the divine Reason, the Logos—even begin to
comprehend the mystery of the divine Reason itself suc-

---

* Blaise Pascal, *Pensées* 423 (London: Penguin Classic, 1995), 127.

cumbing to a human death? Our reason can neither prove
for us nor refute the truth of this mystery. It simply gapes
at the very conception of such a notion. If this mystery
did not in fact take place in reality, what a mystery that
anybody would even conceive it in thought!

Yet, while our reason stands perplexed and even paralyzed before this mystery, a great and strange light begins to dawn in our hearts, a light that had never before
dawned upon this earth before the proclamation of the
saving cross of our Lord Jesus Christ.

The brilliance and warmth of this light is like nothing
else that our hearts have ever encountered. It is a brilliance and warmth infinitely more divine than our highest conceptions of an all-powerful, just, and good God.
It is the brilliance and warmth of the glorious light of the
all-powerful God who became utterly weak for our sake,
the just God whose justice declares itself through infinite
mercy, the good God who willingly becomes the victim of
every evil. When this strange new light strikes our hearts,
our hearts do not merely recognize a truth that far tran-
scends our reason. Our hearts break.

Among the great constellation of mysteries that we
celebrate today, there is the great and strangely wonderful mystery of the breaking of our hearts. How is it that
Zech. 12:10   as we look at the one we have pierced, as we behold the
John 19:37   one who has borne our griefs and carried our sorrows
Isa. 53:4   and was wounded and killed for our sins—how is it that
the breaking of our hearts as we behold all this fills us
John 14:27   with a deep peace that the world can never give us and
even overwhelms us with a joy more profound than any
earthly pleasure?

At the Easter Vigil, we will sing, "Through the Cross,
joy has come into all the world." Tonight, we are already
experiencing the grace-filled mystery that at the heart of

this joy that has come into all the world through the cross is the unutterably sweet and resplendent joy of a broken heart—a heart broken by God's love, broken not because of an unrequited love but because of an unsolicited love, a love undeserved, unlimited, unrestrained.

It is this broken heart of which the psalmist spoke when he said that "a broken and contrite heart God will not spurn." Indeed, how can God spurn such a broken *Ps. 51:17* heart when it is nothing else but the reflection of his own broken heart? And what is this love that breaks our heart except the love poured out upon us from God's own incarnate broken heart, broken by our sins, our lack of love for him, and our neglect of his love for us? Yet, God's broken heart is able to pulse through our human death and love us into indestructible life.

But we can only receive the life-giving love that comes from God's broken heart if we allow our own hearts to be broken by this divine love. We spend practically every moment of our lives trying to fortify our hearts. But, as we celebrate the mystery of our Lord's passion and death, it is fitting and right, it is our duty and our salvation, it is our joy and our peace, to let our hearts be broken. To-night, we receive the grace to let our hearts be torn open, just like the veil of the temple was torn from top to bot- tom, in order to receive the outpouring of the divine love *Matt. 27:51* that led our Lord to the cross and that eternally flows out of his crucified body to all the members of his body in the church.

In the Old Testament prophecy for today's great feast, the prophet Ezekiel announces the mystery of the res- urrection of Israel, a mystery now fulfilled in the body of Christ, which is the church. But a few verses before the reading that we just heard, the prophet Ezekiel also proclaimed the mystery of the life-giving breaking of our hearts when he said, speaking in the name of the Lord, "A new heart I will give you, and a new spirit I will put within you, and I will remove from your body the heart *Ezek. 36:26* of stone and give you a heart of flesh."

When our hearts of stone are broken and replaced by hearts of flesh, the Spirit of God erupts from within *John 7:38* our new hearts, like rivers of living water, and we already, at that point, begin to rise from the dead. My brothers and sisters, this is exactly what is happening now, at this liturgy. Beneath all the beautiful ceremony, the far more beautiful reality is that our hearts are breaking! The infinite compassion of our loving God is breaking our hearts; our hearts of stone are being turned into hearts of flesh; our dried-up bones are pulsating with new life. We are rising from the dead!

Now, what should we do with our brand-new hearts of flesh? First and foremost, and always and at all times and places, we praise the Lord. "Let everything that has *Ps. 150:6* breath praise the Lord," as we just chanted. Let every stony heart that has been broken and changed into a heart of flesh and filled with the breath of the Spirit praise the Lord for his infinite compassion manifested in his life-giving cross.

But we also need to rest. We are undergoing a heart transplant, after all, and that requires rest. Tonight, and tomorrow, and until we celebrate the resurrection of our Lord, it is time to rest in the Lord and to join him in his Sabbath rest. As we just chanted, "Having fulfilled his plan in the Passion, the sovereign of the ages now takes his Sabbath rest in the tomb, granting us a new Sabbath."*

---

* Mother Mary and Kallistos Ware, *The Lenten Triodion* (South Canaan, PA: St. Tikhon's Seminary Press, 2002), 652 (altered).

Tonight and tomorrow, and until we celebrate the resurrection of our Lord, is a time to enter deeply into the grace of the new Sabbath that the Lord granted us by lying in the tomb. It is time for us to enter into the Lord's rest and to partake of this new Sabbath by resting from all our sins, all our vices, our hostilities, our suspicions and jealousies, our betrayals of faith and hope and love. Let us give ourselves a rest from all that, so that we can celebrate the coming festival "not with the leaven of malice and evil, but with the unleavened bread of sincerity and truth."

1 Cor. 5:8

Our new hearts of flesh need rest, the new rest that comes from the new Sabbath in Christ, a Sabbath in which we are freed from the tyranny of all the pharaohs of our sins and vices. It is time for us now to rest with Christ in the tomb; it is time to enjoy the Sabbath rest of dying in Christ. It is time to die in Christ so that we may rise in him.

As we lie with our crucified Lord in the tomb, we know that the world around us wants us to stay dead. The world wants to secure the stone over the Lord's tomb and to silence the proclamation of his resurrection. But that will never happen. No quantity of guards or stratagems can secure that tomb, for—as we said many times in the Lenten liturgy of St. Basil—"it is impossible for the principle of life to be held by corruption." So, we do not have to worry that if we enter the tomb with Christ, we will not come out. Quite the opposite, the more we enter the tomb, the more we die in Christ, the more we partake of the new Sabbath rest that he offers us today, the more secure is our hope of rising with him.

Matt. 27:66

So, my brothers and sisters, let us seize the grace set before us in these most holy days. Let us rejoice in the breaking of our hearts as we behold our crucified Lord;

let us find rest with Christ in the tomb; and let us wait for him to summon us once more to the glorious vision of his resurrection.

May all this come to pass for us through the grace of our crucified Lord Jesus Christ, and the love of God the Father, and the communion of their all-holy, good, and life-giving Spirit, now and always and forever and ever. Amen.

The New Song of the Cross

Ezekiel 37:1–14; 1 Corinthians 5:6–8;
Galatians 3:13–14; Matthew 27:62–66

Brothers and sisters who are dearly beloved in Christ Jesus our Lord:

In the last minutes of his earthly life, when our Lord Jesus was hanging on the cross, he cried out, "Father, forgive them, for they do not know what they are doing." *Luke 23:34* Today, as we enter once again, by the power of the Spirit, into the mystery of our Lord's saving passion, it is true of us also that we do not know what we are doing. The more we try to describe and understand what we are doing, the more incomprehensible it all becomes.

According to the prayers we have been reciting and chanting, what we are doing tonight is celebrating the human murder of God. We are grieving the death of the Author of Life and seeking refuge from our own death in his life-giving death. What we are doing tonight is peering into the deepest darkness of all the evil of the world, only to be overwhelmed by the blinding light of God's saving goodness shining from the tomb of Christ. Tonight, this blinding light shines brightly into the dark-

ness of our hearts and our hearts cannot comprehend it.
Our hearts are mystically illumined and strangely warmed
by this light and yet we still cannot comprehend it. Forgive us, Father, for we do not know what we are doing
as we celebrate the mystery of the human death of your
eternal Son.

Yet, as much as we are unable to understand this mystery, we are able to proclaim it in song, as we have been
doing in the strangely beautiful chants that we just sang. In
singing these lamentations, we are bringing to fulfillment
tonight the exhortation of the psalmist when he cried out,
"Sing to the LORD a new song, sing to the LORD all the
earth. Sing to the LORD, bless his name; tell of his salvation from day to day. Declare his glory among all the
nations."

Ps. 96:1–3

What is this "new song" that the psalmist is talking
about? The psalmist was speaking in the Spirit about a
mystery that he himself likely did not fully comprehend,
a mystery that is being fulfilled among us, and by us, in
this liturgy. According to this mystery, "new song" does
not just mean "another song"; it means a completely new
and up-to-that point unimaginable kind of song. Because
the psalmist did not fully comprehend the mystery that
he himself was declaring, the song that he himself sings
to the Lord is not much different than the old song that
God's people have always sung to the Lord. He cries out
in song,

> Honor and majesty are before him;
> strength and beauty are in his sanctuary.
> Ascribe to the LORD, O families of the
>   peoples,
> Ascribe to the LORD glory and strength.

Ps. 96:6–7

Now, that is a truly beautiful song to sing to the Lord, but it is not really the new song that the psalmist himself was inspired to speak about. This new song is the song we are singing tonight. It is a song that sings not only of God's honor and majesty but of God's dishonor and humiliation. It is a song that sings not only of God's strength and beauty and glory but of God's weakness and disfigurement and debasement. The new song sings of God, the King of Glory, appearing as "one who had no form or majesty that we should look at him, nothing in his appearance that we should desire him . . . despised and rejected by others"; a mere "man of suffering and acquainted with infirmity, as one from whom others hide their faces." This *Isa. 53:2–3* is the new song we are singing tonight to our crucified Lord, a song that sings of the God who willingly accepted death at the hands of his own creation so that he could renew it through his suffering love.

Although the full melody of this new song was not revealed before the coming of Christ, and indeed it was not fully revealed until his death and resurrection, strains of that melody were sounding throughout the history of our salvation. The God who revealed himself to our forefathers and mothers, the God of Abraham, Isaac, and Jacob, was always a God of infinite compassion, a God whose honor and majesty never manifested itself as aloofness from human suffering.

This is the God who, when our first parents disobeyed him and hid themselves from him, went out looking for them and saying, "Where are you?" God's first response *Gen. 3:9* to human sin, that awful sin that began the long and still-continuing nightmare of our alienation from him, was not a sentence of punishment but the searching cry of a rejected lover: "Where are you?"

This is the God who, from the beginning, allowed the horror of human violence to enter into the abode of his heavenly sanctuary, the God who permitted the cry of spilled human blood to infiltrate the song of the angelic choirs that sing to his glory without ceasing. When the first murderer, Cain, killed his brother, Abel, this is the God who said, "Listen, your brother's blood is crying out to me from *Gen. 4:10* the ground." How much crying out of human blood has our merciful God been listening to from that time to this!

This is the God whose honor and majesty never shielded him from being "grieved to the heart" by human evil, as Scripture tells us: "The LORD saw that the wickedness of humankind was great in the earth and that every inclination of the thoughts of their hearts was only evil continually. And the LORD was sorry that he had made hu-*Gen. 6:5–6* mankind on the earth and it grieved him to his heart."

In short, this was the God who always took note and still takes note of every instance of human suffering, as another psalm testifies to us: "You take note of trouble and grief, that you may take it into your hands; the helpless commit themselves to you; you have been the helper of *Ps. 10:14* the orphan." In this psalm, the psalmist sings of the Lord's bountiful compassion, and the entire history of salvation is filled with that same song in praise and wonderment at the Lord's infinitely tender compassion.

But there was one melody line still missing from that song, whose revelation initiated the "new song" that we are singing tonight. The old song sang of the Lord's infinitely forgiving compassion, his unbroken solidarity with human suffering and with the victims of every evil. But it did not sing of the Lord's compassion and solidarity reaching the point of God letting himself be personally the victim of all human evil and all human sin.

It was in order to give us the melody and the words for that new song that the Father sent his only begotten Son into the world to become the universal victim of all sin and evil, to purify all human evil and sin in his holy love, to intercede for every sinner and evildoer, to console and glorify every victim of sin and evil, to become in himself a Passover from the unspeakable horror of sin to the ineffable beauty and joy of divine glory.

And so, my brothers and sisters, this is the new song that we are singing tonight, in fulfillment of the psalmist's exhortation: "Sing to the LORD a new song, sing to the LORD all the earth. . . . Tell of his salvation from day to day. Declare his glory among all the nations." *Ps. 96:1–3*

When we sing this new song, we do not only celebrate our salvation; we receive our salvation. Indeed, without singing this song, we can have no part in the Lord's salvation. I do not mean that we must sing these exact words that we just sang in our beautiful lamentations in order to be saved. What is necessary is to love and glorify the Lord's passion, with our whole heart, our whole mind, all our strength. To sing the new song to the Lord means to *Matt. 22:37* love our Lord Jesus Christ in his suffering, which is what we are doing tonight.

There is no salvation for us if we do not sing this song because we cannot have access to the saving benefits of the Lord's suffering love if we do not love the Lord in his suffering. It is only by loving the love that saves us that we can be saved by that love. The love that saves us is God's suffering love that was fulfilled for us on the cross. How can we receive the fruits of that love if we do not love the love that bears these fruits?

There was a disciple of the Lord, whose name was Johann Sebastian Bach, who knew very well how to sing the

Lord's new song. In one of his cantatas, he puts to music
the following words:

> Jesus, your Passion
> is for me pure joy.
> Your wounds, your crown and scorn
> Are my heart's pasture.*

I do not know if either the writer of these words or
Bach himself, who put them to music, was thinking of
Psalm 23 when they composed this music. But I think it
is very fitting to apply these words to that beloved and
eternally comforting psalm, which begins with the words
that I am sure you all know and love:

Ps. 23:1–3

> The LORD is my shepherd, I shall not want.
> He makes me lie down in green pastures,
> He leads me beside waters of rest,
> He restores my soul.

In this case, too, I believe that the psalmist is declaring a mystery that he does not fully comprehend. This
psalmist, inspired by the Spirit to sing these words, did
not yet fully know the contents of the new song that we
are singing tonight. He did not know that the Lord, our
Shepherd, would take human flesh in order to lay down
John 10:11 his life for the sheep. He did not know that this Shepherd would allow himself to be slain and torn to pieces by
his own deranged sheep who had acquired the character
of vicious wolves. And how could this inspired psalmist

---

* Cantata BWV 182; my translation from the German: "Jesu, deine
Passion ist mir lauter Freude, deine Wunden, Kron und Hohn meines
Herzens Weide."

have imagined that the "green pastures" to which the Lord would lead his sheep to restore their souls would be his saving passion that destroys sin and conquers death and redeems all sadness and fulfills all joy?

Brothers and sisters, as we await the saving manifestation of our Lord's glorious resurrection, may our hearts graze lovingly in the green pastures of the Lord's life-giving passion. May the Spirit wash over us like rest-giving waters as we observe the glorious Sabbath in which our broken world has been renewed. And may our souls be restored in the risen Lord, and our dead bones come to life again, as we continue to sing the beautiful antiphon *Ezek. 27:4–5* from our Holy Thursday prayers:

> We worship your Passion, O Lord,
> Show us soon your Glorious Resurrection.

EASTER VIGIL

LIFE UNMIXED

Mark 16:1–8; Acts 1:1–9; John 1:1–17

My brothers and sisters who are dearly beloved in Christ
Jesus our risen Lord: Christ is risen!

> Christ is risen! He is truly risen!
> *Christos Anesti! Alēthos Anesti!*
> *Al-Masih Qam! Haqan Qam!*
> *Christo ha resucitado! Verdaderamente ha
>   resucitado!*
> *Christo Ressuscitou!—Em Verdade Ressuscitou!*
> *Khristos voskres—voistina voskres!**

We began our paschal canon on this glorious night,
as we reentered the chapel, by singing: "It is the day of
Resurrection. Let us be radiant, O people!"

---

* It is a Byzantine tradition to exchange the greeting of "Christ is
risen! He is truly risen!" in various languages during the Easter season,
beginning with the Easter liturgy. Along with the traditional Greek rendering, the above greetings correspond to the native languages of various members of the congregation to whom this homily was delivered:
English, Arabic, Spanish, Portuguese, and Ukrainian.

On this night in which we partake of the everlasting day of the Lord's resurrection, we are radiant indeed. We are radiant because the foundation of our faith, which is often hidden from our conscious awareness because of the cares of the world and our own sinfulness, is once again revealed to us. This foundation, which is the resurrection of our Lord, is also the true revelation of the fullness of happiness for which every human heart yearns.

Today, as we celebrate the resurrection of our Lord, we plunge once again into the mystery of this fulfillment of our happiness. Today, through the sacramental grace of this liturgy, we know what real happiness is and we know how true happiness can be.

Every other day, every other moment in our lives that is darkened by the forgetfulness of the radiant light of the Lord's resurrection, we find ourselves in mortal combat with death itself. We do not always recognize that our struggle is with death. We struggle with fear, with despair, with disappointment, with physical pain, with sadness and humiliation and loneliness and hatred, and with the self-destruction that comes from all our sins. But all the time, it is really death against which we struggle, for all these are simply the messengers and representatives of death. But, today, in this holy time and place, in this liturgy, we are snatched away from our imprisonment to the forces of darkness and are placed securely back on the foundation of the good news, the best news, of our faith in the Lord Jesus, who has risen from the dead.

Today, the power of the risen Christ is sacramentally renewed for us and makes us recognize again what true happiness is. We know now and we will know forever that real and true and perfect happiness is simply the resurrection of our Lord Jesus Christ. Absolutely nothing else is true happiness, but that alone. We know now and we will know forever that real and true and perfect life is simply the resurrection of our Lord Jesus Christ. Absolutely nothing else is true life, but that alone. Everything else is life mixed with death. How wearisome, how sad, how endlessly disappointing is this constant life mixed with death, pleasure mixed with bitterness, hope mixed with despair, calm mixed with terror, love mixed with hatred, which is the stuff of our daily lives.

But, today, we see and feel and experience something different: Pure, true life, all by itself, unmixed with death, the risen life of our Lord Jesus Christ. What is this life, the true life, the pure life, the source of everything living? It is not just a substance, it is not stuff. This life, this true life, this pure life, the source of everything living is a person called Jesus. This true pure life is a person, a divine person who is also a human person, who alone contains in his person true divine life and true human life. Today, this life unmixes itself from everything contrary to it and what we see is nothing but the pure radiance of true life. Today, we discover that this pure radiance of life is also nothing but love: the love that "moved the sun and stars,"* the love that became flesh in order to move our hearts of stone and turn them into hearts of flesh, the love that suffered death in order to show us that it cannot die, the love that rose from the dead in order to raise us into itself.

So, how can we contain our joy, my brothers and sisters, on this day in which creation is perfected forever and ever? Yes, it is true that the rest of our lives still appear to be full of that wearisome mixture of happiness and sadness, joy and grief, pleasure and pain, confidence and fear, love and hatred. But the grace that is offered us today, the grace of the risen Christ, is the power to get rid of that

* Dante, *Paradiso*, Canto 33.

awful mixture and replace it with the pure unmixed life of the Lord's Passover.

We no longer have to just accept this mixture, as if our happiness and sadness are equally valid, as if our joy and grief have equal authority, as if love and hatred are equally legitimate, as if life and death are two equal antagonists. The risen Lord has not only shown us that happiness and joy and life have the final word; he has become for us the way for passing over, at every moment of our lives, from sadness to happiness, from grief to joy, from death to life. This is the Passover of his resurrection to which he invites us today.

And that is why today we sing: "Our Passover, Christ the Redeemer, is revealed to us today as a noble Passover. This is a new and holy Passover, a mystical Passover . . . a glorious Passover, a Passover for the faithful, a Passover that sanctifies all believers."*

So, let us embrace this Passover, my brothers and sisters, today and for all the remaining days of our lives. Let us now approach the holy table and replenish ourselves in the Passover meal that the Lord serves us now and for all eternity, the meal that fills us with true and perfect happiness. This is the meal in which we are offered the food and drink that give us the true and perfect life that is completely unmixed with death, the body and blood of the risen Lord who gives us the power to pass over from darkness to light, from sorrow to joy, from death to life. May the grace of this holy Passover meal make our whole lives an unmixed offering of praise and thanksgiving to the one and only true and living and almighty and all-loving God, the Father, the Son, and the Holy Spirit. Amen.

---

* *The Pentecostarion*, Service Books of the Byzantine Churches (Boston, MA: Sophia Press, 2002), 1:22.

HE IS NOT HERE, HE IS RISEN

Mark 16:1–8; Acts 1:1–9; John 1:1–17

Brothers and sisters who are dearly beloved in Jesus Christ our risen Lord:

> Christ is risen! He is truly risen!
> *Christos Anesti! Alēthōs Anesti!*
> *Al-Masih Qam! Haqan Qam!*
> *Christo ha resucitado! Verduderamente ha
>   resucitado!*
> *Christo Ressuscitou!—Em Verdade Ressuscitou!*
> *Khristos voskres—voistina voskres!*

It has been two long years since we have been able to celebrate together, as the Byzantine Catholic Community at Notre Dame, this feast of feasts, the resurrection of our Lord Jesus Christ. The past year has been difficult for all of us, though if we are alive here today, then it has gone

---

This sermon was preached at the Easter Vigil of 2021. As the first line of the sermon indicates, it was the first celebration of Easter for our community since the outbreak of the Covid pandemic.

better for us than for many. May the souls of the departed rest in peace and may their loved ones find consolation in the Spirit of our risen Lord. I remember that last year around Easter, several people expressed to me that even after Easter, it felt like it was still Lent. It felt like Easter hadn't really come in 2020. Perhaps it still feels a bit like that today. With respect to the pandemic, it seems that we can now see some light at the end of the tunnel, but there is still considerable tunnel to go through. But apart from the pandemic, we should not neglect the ongoing suffering of so many people who struggle daily with physical and mental suffering, with poverty and oppression, and countless other trials and tribulations. Easter by itself is not going to make that all go away.

So, what then exactly are we celebrating tonight? What is the reason for our joy? If we are joyful, by the grace of God, is our joy truly justified in the face of the ongoing suffering of the world? Where is the risen Lord in all this suffering?

My brothers and sisters, the risen Lord is not here!

I am sorry to scandalize you by saying this. But when I say to you, "the risen Lord is not here," I am simply proclaiming to you the resurrection in the same terms in which it was just proclaimed by the angel in the gospel. The angel says to the women who came with spices to *Matt. 28:6* anoint Jesus at the tomb, "He is risen. He is not here." When they entered the tomb, they did not immediately see the risen Lord. He was gone and the angel confirmed his absence: "He is risen. He is not here." So, it is odd, is it not, that the absence of the Lord—"he is not here"—is part of the resurrection proclamation of the angel. In fact, in the Gospel of Luke, the same scene is retold, and this time the proclamation of the absence of Jesus comes first.

The angels say: "Why do you seek the living one among *Luke 24:5*
the dead? He is not here. He is risen."

So, what I am trying to say to you, my brothers and
sisters, is the very same thing: "He is not here. He is risen."
We have all heard this proclamation many times. And yet,
we are prone to just skip over the "he is not here" part —
so much so, that you were startled and perhaps alarmed
when I said that part all by itself. And yet, "he is not here"
is integral to the real and truly authentic proclamation of
the resurrection of our Lord—the proclamation of this
good news, this best news ever, as absolutely real and concrete and something that can and must be experienced by
every Christian.

What does it mean, then, to say that "he is not here"
as part of our proclamation of the resurrection? It means
that the manifestation of our Lord's resurrection cannot
be found and should not be looked for in the automatic
transformation of external circumstances. The risen presence of the Lord cannot be properly apprehended if our
focus is restricted to the realm of merely perishable things.
And by the realm of merely perishable things, I mean the
whole world. This whole world is, in a very real sense,
a tomb; as they say, no one who enters it gets out alive.
We all try to make our little corner of the tomb as pretty
and comfortable as possible and we try to cover over the
stench of death with all kinds of spices and fragrance, and
that is all natural and even good in itself.

This is what the women in the gospel today were doing
too. But then they received the proclamation of the resurrection: "He is not here. He is risen. Why do you seek the
living one among the dead?" My brothers and sisters, today *Luke 24:5*
we receive the same proclamation and the same question
and the same challenge. If we want to truly experience the

resurrection of our Lord, as a reality and not just a fantasy and a feel-good story, we have to look beyond the tomb, beyond the whole tomb of this whole world. And this is exactly the instruction we have been given by someone who did see the risen Lord, who tells us: "If you have been raised with Christ, seek the things that are above, where *Col. 3:1* Christ is seated at the right hand of God."

If we just keep focused on the tomb, we might see some signs and indications that Christ has been there, we might even have some stimulating conversations with angels, but we will not see the risen Lord. We will not apprehend his risen presence. Because he is not here; he is risen.

But if we look beyond the tomb, if we allow ourselves to be lifted up in the Spirit to the things above where Christ is seated at the right hand of the Father, we will experience his resurrection. We will see his glory, "the *John 1:14* glory of the Father's only Son, full of grace and truth," and we will receive from the fullness of his life grace upon *John 1:16* grace. We will behold the glory of his resurrection with unveiled faces, and we will be changed into his risen like-*2 Cor. 3:18* ness from one degree of glory to another. We will enter into the heavenly sanctuary by the new and living way which he opened for us through his risen flesh; we will enter through the inner shrine where the risen Lord has *Heb. 10:19–20* entered, as a forerunner on our behalf.

But what about the tomb then? Is there nothing to do in the tomb of this world except have spiritual visions of the risen Lord and sit around waiting to die? No, God forbid!

First of all, if we plant our hearts and minds within the mystery of the risen Lord, we ourselves are no longer in the tomb. A tomb is a piece of earth that encloses the dead. We said that, in a sense, this whole world is a tomb since it eventually encloses all of us as dead. But our Lord's resurrection has destroyed the finality of this power of enclosure and so this world is, in reality, no longer a tomb for us who have been raised up with Christ. Instead, it is a garden in which we all fall as seed that can bear much fruit, even the fruit of eternal life and everlasting glory. Second, we do not just sit around waiting to die and be resurrected. Nothing can be further from the gospel. Many other religions hold out the promise of resurrection after death. But this is not our Christian faith, which is founded on the resurrection of our Lord, an event that has already occurred in the midst of history and is meant to recur at every moment of our lives. Since we have been baptized into the Lord's Passover from death and resurrection, every moment of our lives is a Passover from death to life, from earth to heaven, from life in the world as tomb to life in the world as the garden that bears the fruit of eternal life.

John 12:24

It does not matter what our circumstances are— whether we are passing through poverty or wealth, sickness or health, pandemic or mass vaccinations, political turmoil or social stability, contentment or distress— whatever we may pass through on the surface of this world while our true life is hidden with Christ in God, the reality of our life in the risen Lord is that we are already passing over to eternal life, through Christ our present and eternal Passover.

Col. 3:3

This same Christ, our Passover sacrifice, now offers himself to us as the food and drink of our Passover journey in this most holy Eucharist that we offer tonight as a sharing in the grace of his resurrection. At the risk of trying your patience one more time, I will say again that even in the Eucharist, we can say of our risen Lord, "He is not here." If we look at the bread simply as bread, then the presence of the risen Lord is not here. Indeed, once this bread has been consecrated to the Lord, the bread itself will not be here as mere bread. Because of the risen presence of our risen Lord, the bread will pass over into the reality of his resurrected flesh. And if we look at the wine simply as wine, then the risen Lord is not here. And the wine itself will not be here, as mere wine, once it has been consecrated. Because of the risen presence of our risen Lord, this wine will pass over into the reality of his resurrected blood, and the power of his life and death and resurrection.

Let us now eat and drink this Passover meal. As we pass over from the consumption of mere bread and wine to the partaking of the life-giving death and risen life of the Lord, let us pass over from this mortal life to eternal life and eternal joy and eternal glory through Christ our risen Lord, through whom we give eternal praise in the Holy Spirit to our loving and life-giving and most gracious heavenly Father, now and always and forever and ever. Amen.

BE REALISTIC,
CHRIST IS RISEN!

Mark 16:1–8; Acts 1:1–9; John 1:1–17

Brothers and sisters who are dearly beloved in Christ Jesus our risen Lord:

> Christ is risen! He is truly risen!
> *Christos Anesti! Alēthōs Anesti!*
> *Al-Masih Qam! Haqan Qam!*
> *Christo ha resucitado! Verdaderamente ha*
>   *resucitado!*
> *Christo Ressuscitou!—Em Verdade Ressuscitou!*
> *Khristos voskres—voistina voskres!*

At the paschal proclamation that we sang outside the chapel tonight, we chanted the verse from the psalm, "This is the day that the Lord has made. Let us rejoice and be glad in it." And when we came back into the chapel, *Ps. 118:24* we sang, "It is the day of Resurrection, let us be radiant, O people." Indeed, tonight we are radiant with the light of this new day that the Lord has made for us to rejoice and be glad in. It was for the sake of this glorious day of the resurrection of our Lord Jesus Christ that every other day was made by the Lord. It was in order to make us perfectly radiant on this perfect day that the eternal Radiance of *Heb. 1:3* the Father's light, which enlightens everyone who comes *John 1:9* into the world, itself came into the world and enlightened our darkness with the glory of God's only begotten Son, a *John 1:14* glory full of grace and truth.

My brothers and sisters, some of you who have heard me tell the story of my meeting for the first time with the great then-retired and very old Melkite Archbishop Joseph Tawil. That meeting took place during the Easter service and when I greeted him after the service with the traditional greeting, "Christ is risen!" he shocked me by responding, "Are you sure?" I was so startled that I thought that either I had misheard him or he had misheard me. So, again, I repeated, as clearly as I could, "Christ is risen," and again, he repeated, just as clearly, "Are you sure?" At that moment, as I looked at him looking at me with a pure simplicity and a sincerity that was devoid of any trace of false piety, I felt that I knew completely what he wanted to say to me. He was affectionately but also sternly presenting me with a challenge and an ultimatum: "Either fully own and fully commit to this strange thing that you are saying or don't say it at all. Make sure you really mean it before you say it. Are you sure that Christ is risen?"

Every Easter since that time, I remember that encounter. Every Easter, I feel the challenge of that ultimatum. Am I sure that Christ is risen? What does it mean to be sure about that? What does it mean to fully own this strange proclamation and to fully commit to it?

This year, as I grapple again with this challenge, it strikes me that what is at stake in this challenge is what we can call "Easter realism." What is Easter realism? It is simply to see all of reality in the light of Easter, to see the resurrection of Christ as the key that not only opens the Scriptures for us but reveals to us the ultimate meaning and ultimate goal of all reality. If the resurrection of Christ is the key to the meaning of all Scripture, and if Scripture is the key to the meaning of all reality, then the resurrection of Christ is the key to all reality. This means that for those of us who accept the reality of the resurrection of Christ, to "be realistic" means to think of reality first and foremost in relation to the resurrection of Christ. This is the essence of "Easter realism."

It says something significant about the human condition that whenever people admonish each other to "be realistic," this admonition inclines toward pessimism and the lowering of expectations. No one says, "Be realistic, all your troubles will be resolved and everything will turn out wonderfully." When someone tells you to "be realistic," they usually mean that you are being too hopeful, too optimistic, that you are letting your wishes and hopes blind you to the disappointing truths of reality. This tendency to associate "being realistic" with pessimism and low expectations reveals a core belief that reality itself is ultimately deficient. It expresses the deep-seated conviction that objective reality does not correspond to our deepest desires and hopes. Be realistic: things are not the way you would like them to be. Life is not on your side.

But the resurrection of our Lord Jesus Christ reveals to us that this so-called realism of the world is in fact neither true nor real. The resurrection of our Lord Jesus Christ reveals that Life is completely on our side, since the eternal Word of the Father, in whom is life, is completely on our side. He has vanquished death and granted us eternal life, not in some future state after we die, but right now, so that our every moment on this earth can already be inundated with eternal life, so that even our earthly death will be for us a life-giving death, as it was for our risen Lord.

My brothers and sisters, you don't have to wait to die before you can be risen with Christ. You have already been raised with Christ. As the apostle tells us, "God, who is rich in mercy, out of the great love with which he loved us, even *Eph. 2:4–6*   when we were dead through our trespasses, made us alive together with Christ . . . and raised us up with him and seated us with him in the heavenly places in Christ Jesus."

If we believe all this, if we are sure that Christ is risen, if we are sure that God has made us alive together with Christ—with the true life that is in Christ and by which he conquered death—if we are sure that God has already raised us up with him and seated us with him in the heavenly places, so that we are now citizens of heaven even while we travel through this earth; if we are sure of all this, then we have to radically change our way of being realistic.

My brothers and sisters, in the early church, the post-Easter period was a time in which the newly baptized were instructed on the meaning of the sacraments that they were now able to receive for the first time. This instruction was called "mystagogy." But every Easter, all of us, and not only the newly baptized, are invited to an existential mystagogy, a deep and drastic reevaluation and reinterpretation of all aspects of our existence in light of the resurrection of Christ. Every Easter we are invited to "be realistic" in a completely different way than the cynical and hopeless so-called realism of the world that does not know the risen Lord.

For us, to *be realistic* means to raise our expectations rather than to lower them. As the apostle also tells us: "Since you have been raised with Christ, seek the things that are above, where Christ is seated at the right hand *Col. 3:1–2*   of God. Set your minds on things that are above, not on things that are on earth."

For us, to *be realistic* means to be confident that every step of our journey in this earthly life is bringing us closer to the fullness of our participation in Christ's final victory over sin and death.

For us, to *be realistic* is to recognize that, in the light of Christ's resurrection, all our deepest desires and hopes correspond to the deepest core of reality, which is God's infinite goodness that has become fully embodied for us in the resurrection of our Lord Jesus Christ. Life *is* completely on our side, as long as we are on the side of the true life that has been poured out into the world through the resurrection of our Lord Jesus Christ.

If we are tempted to despair when we see how evil seems to reign supreme in our world, we have to *be realistic* with genuine Easter realism—and recognize that evil does not wield real power in the world. Rather, our risen Lord is allowing evil to come out of hiding and expose itself so that it can be recognized as evil and utterly rejected by God's elect, so that when evil manifests itself it can be *Ps. 36:2* ambushed by the power of his resurrection. Just as our Lord entered through the fullness of life by overcoming evil and death through his suffering love, he is giving us an opportunity to overcome the evil of the world through the power of his cross. Soon, he will come and manifest his glory to the whole world. But, for now, he desires to manifest his risen glory through us, through our overcoming evil by the power of his cross.

When we are overwhelmed by our own sufferings, we have to *be realistic*, and recognize that, as the apostle tells us, "our present sufferings are not worth comparing with the glory about to be revealed to us." And we have already *Rom. 8:18* seen this glory, haven't we, the glory as of God's only Son? We are seeing this glory as we celebrate this Divine Liturgy, are we not?

When we become fearful at the prospect of our own death, we have to *be realistic*, and remember that our resurrection faith tells us that our risen Lord subjected himself to death "so that through death he might destroy the power of death . . . and free those who all their lives were held in slavery by the fear of death." We who have been raised up with Christ and made alive together with Christ know that death is no longer our master but our servant, who has been commissioned to lead us to the risen Lord. It is simply not realistic, my brothers and sisters in Christ, for those of us who have been raised up with Christ through his life-giving death, to fear death.

Heb. 2:14–15

My brothers and sisters in the risen Lord, we have ahead of us forty days of grace to be instructed by the risen Lord in the mystagogy of Easter realism. We have forty days to learn what it means to be sure of the message that we proclaim whenever we say, "Christ is risen! He is truly risen." We have forty days of grace to train ourselves to be realistic in the mode of Easter realism.

Let us now begin this joyful instruction in Easter realism by enjoying a festive meal with our risen Lord. Let us also be realistic about what exactly we are doing and what gifts are being offered to us as we partake of this joyful banquet. In the fullness of Easter realism, let us dare to believe that what is offered to us in this feast is really and truly the precious and holy body and blood of our risen Lord, Jesus Christ.

May this real and true participation in the life of our risen Lord fill us with an unshakeable Easter realism that we may be able to see all of reality in light of its fulfillment in the resurrection of our Lord Jesus Christ, through the Holy Spirit whom the Lord has promised to pour out anew on us in the coming feast of Pentecost, to the glory of God our Father. Amen.

EASTER SEASON

The Peace
of the Resurrection

Acts 5:12–20; John 20:19–31

Brothers and sisters who are dearly beloved in Christ Jesus our risen Lord:

In our first Scripture reading from the Vigil of the Resurrection of our Lord, the apostle Luke tells us that "after his suffering [our Lord] presented himself alive to [his disciples] by many convincing proofs, appearing to them during forty days and speaking to them about the kingdom of God." During these forty days of the Easter season, *Acts 1:3* as we rejoice in the resurrection of our Lord and await the fulfillment of his promise to renew in us the outpouring of his Holy Spirit at Pentecost, the risen Lord wants to present himself alive to us by many convincing proofs, as he did to the first disciples. Our risen Lord wishes to appear to us during these forty days and to speak to us about the kingdom of God, which has been established on earth through his resurrection from the dead.

And just as we read in the gospel for today's liturgy, the risen Lord comes into our midst today, at this liturgy,

John 20:19 and says, "Peace be with you." Just as he was able to appear to his first disciples, even though the doors were closed, so now he is able to appear to us, even though the doors of our physical senses are closed to the perception of his glorified body. At this liturgy, our risen Lord enters past the closed doors of our physical senses and appears to us in the power of his Spirit and says, "Peace be with you."

This peace that the Lord offers us is not a mere calmness or tranquility or quietness. In the Gospels, our Lord never says "Peace be with you" to his disciples except in the context of his resurrection. I am sure that Jesus was a peaceful person and projected calmness and tranquility and serenity. But he did not go around saying "Peace be with you" as just a regular greeting. He does not begin his Sermon on the Mount, for example, by saying, "Peace be with you." The only time before his resurrection that Jesus says "Peace be with you"—or something equivalent to that—is in his final discourse to his disciples in the Gospel of John, and in that case, he is speaking with a view to his death and resurrection; he says, "Peace I leave with you; my peace I give to you. . . . Do not let your hearts be troubled and do not let them be afraid. You heard me say to you, 'I am going away, and I am coming to you.' If you loved me, *John 14:27–28* you would rejoice that I am going to the Father."

The fact that Jesus only offers the greeting of peace to his disciples in the context of the resurrection means that this peace he offers is actually the peace of the resurrection. It is the peace of Christ's final victory over sin and death. This is the peace that overcomes the enmity *Rom. 8:7* between God and sinful humanity, the peace that breaks *Eph. 2:14* down the walls of division between human beings and *Rom. 12:5* unites all people in the one body of the risen Lord, the *1 John 5:4* peace through which we conquer the evil of the world and *2 Cor. 5:19* are reconciled to God. This is the peace of the resurrection through which the things of earth have been united with the things of heaven through Christ's rising from the earth and ascending to heaven.

It is this peace of the power of our Lord's resurrection that we exchange at every liturgy when the priest says, "Peace be with you," and you answer back, "And with your spirit."* When we exchange this blessing of peace, we are blessing each other with the power of Christ's resurrection. In this exchange, it is the risen Lord himself who stands among us, even though the doors of our physical senses may be closed to his risen glory, and he says to us at every liturgy, "Peace be with you. The peace of my resurrection be with you." During these forty days of the Easter season, the Lord wishes to renew in us this peace of his resurrection. He wants to enter past the closed doors of our senses and assure us, through the Holy Spirit, that it is really he, the risen One, who stands in our midst and gives us the peace of his resurrection through the liturgical exchange of peace between the priest and the people at every liturgy.

In granting us the peace of his resurrection, the risen Lord also heals and enlivens our faith in the reality of his resurrection, just as he did in the case of Thomas. Through the proclamation of today's gospel, the risen Lord is asking each of us to hand over to him our resurrection faith for healing and renewal, so that our faith may be filled with the peace of his resurrection.

My brothers and sisters, faith is a gift from God, and faith in the resurrection of our Lord Jesus Christ is no exception. Our faith in the resurrection of our Lord Jesus Christ is itself the result of the power of his resurrection. We

---

* In the Byzantine liturgy, the exchange of "Peace be with you / And with your spirit" is recurrent through the liturgy.

cannot maintain and nurture this faith by our own power, and we can never take it for granted. Faith is not something we can just put in a safe deposit box in the bank and be done with it. We can only have a true and living faith if we continually offer this faith to God for healing and renewal, and this is something we especially need to do every Easter. Therefore, the point of today's gospel is not for us to have contempt for Thomas's lack of faith and to feel superior to him. Rather, the risen Lord is asking each of us today, "What will it take for you to have a true and living faith in my resurrection? What will it take for you to be 'not unbelieving but believing'? What will it take for you to perceive my risen glory and to say, 'My Lord and my God'?"

John 20:27–28

Thomas was very clear about what it would take for him to believe and he plainly stated his terms: "Unless I see the mark of the nails in his hands, and put my finger in the mark of the nails and my hand into his side, I will not believe." We see in today's gospel that the Lord accepted the terms that Thomas stipulated. He did not just meet Thomas halfway; he met Thomas exactly where he was and healed his faith and filled it with the peace of his resurrection. For most of us, the problem with our faith is not that we stipulate terms for our belief and demand that these terms be met by the Lord, the way Thomas did. Most of us have the opposite problem: we do not demand or even request anything for the maintenance of our faith, but neither do we let our faith make real demands on us.

John 20:25

A priest friend of mine once told me that once he was presiding at a wedding of one of his nephews. You know that at weddings, a lot of people come to church who don't attend regularly. Apparently, that was the case with one of my friend's relatives who came forward to receive Communion. When the priest offered him the host, saying, "the body of Christ," this person answered, "No problem!" Now, it is quite possible that if you were to take this young man aside and ask him, "Do you believe that this host is really the body of Christ?" he would say, "Sure, whatever; no problem." But is that really faith? If someone says to us, "Christ is risen," and we say, "He is truly risen!" but our real inner response is, "No problem," is that really faith in the resurrection of our Lord Jesus Christ?

The reason that this would not be real faith is that real and genuine faith impels us to a living relationship with the object of our faith. To have real faith in God is to be impelled to have a living relationship with God. You do not have real faith in God if you do not have a burning desire to see God, to feel God, to touch God, to speak to God, and to listen to God. In the same way, to have real faith in the risen Lord is to be impelled to seek an encounter with the risen Lord, to see and touch and feel the risen Lord. That's what Thomas got right.

So, my brothers and sisters, today, the risen Lord stands among us and says, "Peace be with you." He offers us the peace of his resurrection and he also asks us to hand over to him our faith in his resurrection for healing and renewal. He does not want us to respond to the proclamation of his resurrection by saying, "No problem." He wants us to have a real encounter with him, in his risen glory, as one who is fully alive, who wants to share with us the fullness of his life and who wants us to share this fullness of life with all the world. The sure sign that we have received the peace of the resurrection and that our faith in the risen Lord is genuine is that we are conscious of a mission to proclaim the resurrection to all the world. As the risen Lord says to his disciples, he says also to us: "As the Father has sent me, so I send you." And the instruction of *John 20:21* the angel to the apostles also applies to us: "Go . . . and tell the people the whole message of this life." And that is *Acts 5:20* why we proclaim the gospel in different languages on this Sunday, as an acknowledgement that we have accepted and embraced this mission.*

My brothers and sisters, our risen Lord is present with us today at this liturgy and he is offering us the peace of his resurrection, the healing and renewal of our faith in his resurrection, and the invitation to proclaim to the whole world the fullness of life that can only be found in him.

He offers us the fullness of this life now under the signs of bread and wine. May the closed doors of our earthly senses be opened up so that we may spiritually perceive the presence and power of the Lord's life, death, and resurrection under these signs. As we partake of these holy gifts, let us be not unbelieving but believing and let us proclaim, with all the assurance that the Holy Spirit has placed in our hearts, that Jesus Christ, crucified and risen, is our Lord and our God, to the glory of God the Father. Amen.

* In the Byzantine liturgy, the gospel is proclaimed in different languages during Vespers on Easter Sunday and also on the Sunday after Easter. In both cases, the gospel reading of the encounter between Thomas and the risen Lord is read (John 20:19–31).

SUNDAY OF THE MYRRH-BEARING WOMEN

ONLY LOVE CAN SEE
THE RISEN LORD

Acts 6:1–7; Mark 15:43–16:8

Brothers and sisters who are dearly beloved in Christ Jesus our risen Lord:

Today, the Holy Spirit gathers us together to continue our never-ending celebration of the glorious resurrection of our Lord Jesus Christ. In this holy assembly, we recognize the risen Lord in the breaking of bread; we "light the lamps of our souls from the resplendent light of his glorious Resurrection";* we hear from the Lord himself, speaking through the Spirit in our hearts, that all authority on heaven and earth has been given to him and that he will be with us to the end of the age (see Matt. 28:18); and we are instructed by him to devote ourselves to prayer and to proclaiming the Word, and not to neglect to share our joy and our resources with those in need, whether they be widows or refugees or anyone else in need of assurance of the fullness of life that we have received in the risen Lord.   *Acts 6:1–7*

---

* Antiphon for the Sunday of Ointment-Bearing Women.

Now, it might seem, at first, that today's gospel strikes a discordant note in the midst of our Easter celebrations. While the second half of it is a repetition of the first gospel from our Easter Vigil, the first half takes us back to the burial of Jesus. It seems odd to go back now to the burial of Jesus in the midst of our Easter celebration. In fact, overall, the myrrh-bearing women who are the subject of this gospel and whom we commemorate today, do not fare so well in Mark's gospel. They buy spices to anoint Jesus but all that goes to waste; they don't get to anoint him. They get up early and run to the tomb to anoint Jesus's body, but the body is missing. Imagine going to the graveside of some loved one who had just died and finding the grave open and the body gone! Comfort and joy would likely not be our first reaction in that situation. In the gospel we read today, there is no mention of the joy of the myrrh-bearing women. Instead, we are told that they were "alarmed" and "terror . . . seized them." The angels tell them to go and tell the other disciples that Jesus is risen from the dead, but the last words of today's gospel tell us that "they said nothing to anyone, for they were afraid." Yet, for all that, we celebrate the myrrh-bearing women on this third Sunday of the Easter season and so we must ask the Holy Spirit, who inspired this arrangement, to reveal to us the meaning of it.

I believe that at the heart of this meaning is the witness of the myrrh-bearing women to how our earthen vessels can bear the golden treasure of the Easter proclamation, and to how the power of the resurrection manifests itself in our human weakness. Above all, I believe that at the heart of our celebration today is the revelation of the simple but profound truth that we will see the risen Lord if only—and only if—we love Jesus the Christ. We can be afraid, we can be disappointed, we can be alarmed and terrified—all that does not matter in the end. If we love Jesus, we will see and experience his resurrection—not after we die, but even now, even today. If only we let ourselves fall in love with him and remain in love with him—it does not matter how we love him and what aspect of his life and death our love focuses on—in the end, we will see the risen Lord.

If we love Jesus, it does not even matter in the end if our faith in him is defective in some way. Love will heal and elevate our faith. If we love him in his humanity, he will manifest to us his divinity. If we love him in his suffering, he will reveal to us his glory. If we love him in his death, he will show us his resurrection.

The myrrh-bearing women did not have faith in the resurrection of Christ when they went to the tomb. They bought ointment to anoint the dead Jesus, not to greet the risen Lord. But they came to the tomb out of love and in love, a very human love for Jesus. But when the angel told them that Jesus was not in the tomb because he is risen, he was also telling them that their human love for Jesus was not adequate to the reality of Jesus. The angel was telling them that their human love for Jesus had reached its limit with the death of Jesus and now they can love the living Christ only if their hearts follow him into his divinity. Of course, they did not necessarily understand all of this right away. But out of love for Jesus, because love believes all things and hopes all things, they fled from the *1 Cor. 13:7* tomb where they had gone to be with their beloved dead Jesus and went in search of the living and risen Christ. And elsewhere in the gospel, we are told that they did meet the risen Lord and "they came to him, took hold of *Matt. 28:9* his feet, and worshipped him."

My brothers and sisters, loving Jesus Christ is no longer much in vogue. There are many divisions in the church today but there seems to be general agreement to dispense with age-old practices of loving Jesus, of adoring his words and actions and suffering, of savoring his presence with affectionate worship. Today, the myrrh-bearing women recall us to the simple and unfailing way of loving Jesus as the only sure path to seeing the risen Lord. As we continue our celebration of the resurrection of our Lord, the myrrh-bearing women show us that we cannot encounter the risen Lord if we do not love him. The risen Lord, precisely because he is risen, cannot any longer be seen with merely physical eyes: "He is not here"—in the merely *Mark 16:6* physical and material world—"He is risen." He can only be seen with the eyes of the heart, with the eyes of love.

So, if we want to experience the resurrection of Christ this Easter season, we have to fall in love with Jesus once again. It does not matter how we fall in love or what aspect of his presence especially attracts us, or what moment of his life, death, and resurrection attracts our love first.

As long as we fall in love with him, he will lead us through his humanity to his divinity, through his suffering to his glory, through his death to his resurrection. And he will pour out his Spirit on us, the Spirit through which God's love is poured into our heart. He will do all this *1 John 4:19* because it was he who loved us first, who came into our humanity to make his divine love humanly visible and tangible to us, who loved us to death, and loves us into resurrection. All this love, all of God's love for us in Jesus, which enables us to love Jesus in God and to love Jesus as God, is present now at this table of the holy Eucharist.

At the beginning of our gospel today, we read that Joseph of Arimathea came to Pilate and boldly asked for the *Mark 15:43* body of Jesus. When Jesus was dead, Pilate had authority over his body and Joseph of Arimathea had to ask Pilate for his body. But now, no earthly power has authority

over Jesus's body and all authority in heaven and earth belongs to Jesus himself. As we come forward now for holy   *Matt. 28:18*
Communion, we do not ask Pilate or any mere human
being for the body of Jesus. We ask the Father of heaven
and earth for the risen body of his Son. He who did not
withhold his own Son, but gave him up for all of us, will
himself give us the risen body and blood of his own Son.
And will he not with him also give us everything else?   *Rom. 8:32*

He will indeed give us everything else out of love, and
above all the gift of the Holy Spirit through which the love
of God is poured into our hearts and poured out of our
hearts back to God. Through this same Spirit, we will meet
Jesus, our risen Lord—even today, at this liturgy—and we
will love the risen Lord and proclaim forever the victory
of his love, to the glory of God the Father. Amen.

Our Life's Ultimate Goal: Loving Christ

Acts 6:1–7; Mark 15:43–16:8

My brothers and sisters who are dearly beloved in Christ Jesus, our risen Lord:

In preparing for this final liturgy of the academic year, I found myself remembering our first liturgy of the year. At that time, we talked about the difficulty of making new beginnings—whether it be the beginning of the church year or the academic year—in a world that doesn't seem capable of providing the hopeful excitement that should accompany new beginnings. The gospel for that liturgy contained the Great Commandment to love God with all our heart and soul and mind and to love our neighbor as ourselves. At that liturgy, we were consoled in the Spirit by reflecting that we can always find a new beginning in Christ, who is eternally in the beginning, and that the way back to this beginning is love. God, in whom is our beginning, is love, and whenever we love, we are in the beginning, in God.

As we come to the end of another academic year—and for some of us the end of a whole degree program—it is

Matt. 22:37

natural to ask ourselves to what *end* have all our labors been directed over the past year or years. What is the end and goal of all our work and how does that bring us closer to the ultimate end and goal of our existence? And perhaps, we face a similar problem that we faced at the beginning of the year when we considered the difficulty of making new beginnings in our current circumstances. When we consider the various terrible afflictions plaguing our present world, it is hard to envision good and happy endings that would resolve and redeem these afflictions. The world in general does not seem to be oriented to good ends or to accommodate good and happy endings. In such a world, how do we end anything with a sense of real accomplishment and fulfillment?

It might not seem obvious that today's gospel provides us with answers to these questions, but I believe that it does. After all, today's gospel proclaims the good and happy ending that God has arranged for all creation, which is the resurrection of Christ and the renewal of all things in him. But it is especially by considering the myrrh-bearing women, who are the centerpiece of today's liturgy, that we can answer the question of how to envision the end and goal of all our work and how to orient our earthly endings to the final end and goal of our whole existence.

Today's gospel tells us that very early on the first day of the week, after the Sabbath, these women went to the market and bought some aromatic spices and then rushed to the tomb of Jesus in order to anoint his dead body. Why did they do that? To what end? What did they hope to accomplish by this work and effort?

The answer is: Nothing. Nothing at all. They did not hope to accomplish anything; they had no expectations of changing anything. What they did, they did out of love of

Christ and for no other reason than simply to express that love without expecting anything at all in return. Jesus, whom they loved, was dead. And they wanted to express their love for him even though, as far as they knew, he was not alive to receive or respond to their expressions of love.

Now, even though the gospel tells us that these myrrh-bearing women were the first to hear the proclamation of the resurrection of Christ, their story leaves us with a strange uneasiness. A good part of that uneasiness has to do precisely with the lack of accomplishment of these women. They neither got to anoint the body of the dead Jesus nor did they actually see him risen. They wanted to express their love for Jesus but he was not there, as either dead or risen, to be the object of their love. The end of their story, as told by the gospel, is that "they said nothing to anyone, for they were afraid." We know, in fact, that this was the original ending of the whole Gospel of Mark. But this ending proved to be so unsatisfying to people that two other endings were added to it afterwards. Both these later endings are canonical Scripture, inspired by the Holy Spirit. But today's reading takes us back to the original ending and so affirms that ending as a genuine proclamation of the good news of the risen Lord. Therefore, we can be confident that today's gospel is capable of answering the question of how we can envision good endings for our labors in this world, in a world that seems to frustrate our hopes for good endings. Indeed, this seemingly unsatisfying ending provides us with a very profound way of understanding the true end and goal of all our earthly work, which is to share in the power of Christ's resurrection by loving Christ without limit.

It might seem that the myrrh-bearing women did not accomplish anything. But, in reality, they were able to enter into the life of the risen Christ simply by the depth of

Mark 16:8

their love for him. We can even truly say that the love that they experienced for the dead Jesus and that they wanted to express by anointing him was the same love that raised Jesus from the dead. The love that they had for Jesus when they went out to anoint him with aromatic spices was a participation in the very same love that the Father poured out on the dead Jesus and by which the Father loved the dead Jesus back to life. Their love was also a sharing in the love of the Holy Spirit, who blends together the love of the Father and the Son and who breathed forth that mutual love into the dead humanity of Jesus and so brought him back to life. And, of course, the love of these women was also the same love that led Jesus to his death in the first place, the same love that led Jesus to purchase for humanity the aromatic spices of his divine life with his own blood. Therefore, by loving Jesus, the myrrh-bearing women were partaking of the very same love that led Jesus to his death and that raised Jesus from death.

It is this limitless love for Christ that is the true end and goal of all our human actions and sufferings. If we have that love, we are already living in the power of Christ's resurrection, even if there seems to be no tangible results for all our work, even if in the eyes of the world, we have accomplished nothing at all. In reality, the only true accomplishment in this world and the next is to attain and express this love. To attain and express this love is the true essence of resurrection empowerment, even if it seems to lead to no earthly result.

My brothers and sisters, we attain and express this true end and goal of our existence at every Divine Liturgy. At every liturgy, we relive the mystery of the myrrh-bearing women's visit to the tomb of Christ. At every liturgy, God our Father fulfills the role of the myrrh-bearing women by coming to the tomb of our sinful mortality and anointing us in the Spirit with the fragrance of the risen Christ. Every incensation during the liturgy partakes of this mystery. At every liturgy, we also assume the role of the myrrh-bearing women by entering into the tomb of the sinful corruption of the whole world, through our prayers and intercessions. At every liturgy, the Holy Spirit empowers us to anoint the whole world with the fragrance of the risen Christ and enables us to offer the whole world as a sweet spiritual fragrance in thanksgiving to God our Father.

My brothers and sisters, just as it is not given to us to know the day or the hour when our Lord will come in glory to usher in a new heaven and a new earth, it is also not given to us to know exactly *how* each of our actions contributes to the enfoldment of the whole world into the new life of Christ's resurrection. But to have a true faith in the resurrection of our Lord is to have a firm conviction that we have been given the power to revivify the whole world through the life-giving fragrance of the risen Christ. Through the Holy Spirit who has been poured out into our hearts and who anoints us with the fragrance of Christ, we have been given the power to love the whole world into resurrection. That is the true goal and end of all of our actions and sufferings. It is not for us to demand immediate evidence of the tangible results of our love. We only need the evidence of a pure conscience that confirms to us, in the Spirit, that like the myrrh-bearing women, we are loving with the same love that raised Jesus from the dead. He who raised Jesus from the dead in love will grant his risen life to all the world through our spreading of that life-giving love to all the world.

As we approach the holy table, let us ask the Lord that, in partaking of his body and blood, we, like the myrrh-bearing women, may truly share in the power of that love that led him to his death and raised him from the dead.

Let us ask the Holy Spirit to enable us to comprehend the
hidden breadth and length and height and depth of the   *Eph. 3:18*
power of Christ's resurrection working through our love
of the risen Lord. And let us ask God our Father to fill us
with all the fullness of God that is contained bodily in the   *Col. 2:9*
risen Christ, who is both our beginning and our eternal
good end. To him and to his eternally beloved Son and to
the Holy Spirit of their love be all glory in the church and
in the world, forever and ever. Amen.

ASCENSION

WE HAVE OUR HEARTS
WITH GOD

Acts 1:1–12; Luke 24:36–53

My brothers and sisters who are dearly beloved in Jesus Christ our Lord:

One of the most sublime and wonderful and truly uplifting moments of the Divine Liturgy is the exchange between the priest and the people before the great eucharistic prayer, which we call the anaphora. At that point, the priest turns to the people and says, "Let us lift up our hearts," and the people respond, "We lift them up to the Lord."

The great sacramental mystery of that moment is revealed in an even clearer way in the Arabic translation of the liturgy. In Arabic, the priest says: *Li narfa' qoloubouna illa-olah.*

Literally, that means, "Let us lift up our hearts on high," which is basically the same as the English, "Let us lift up our hearts." But the people's response is a little bit different. The people don't say, "We lift them up to the Lord." Instead, when the priest says, "Let us lift up our hearts," the people say, "There they are with God (*Ha hiya 'ind al-Rab*)."

Now, of course, you have to imagine this dialogue in the context of the gestures. The priest looks up and says, "Let us lift up our hearts," and the people look up and say, "There they are with God." As if they are pointing to their hearts and saying: "There they are; there are our hearts. They're up there with God."

This beautiful dialogue—so simple and yet so sublime—is one of the most ancient features of all the eucharistic liturgies of the church, in both East and West. If we just look at the most ancient versions of this dialogue, in Greek and Latin, we find that they are actually closer to the Arabic version than to our more modern English versions.

In the Greek, we say:

Anō schōmen tas kardias. Echomen pros ton Kyrion.
(Let us have our hearts on high. We have them with the Lord.)

Similarly, in the Latin:

Sursum corda. Habemus ad Deum. (Up with our hearts. We have them unto God.)

I am drawing your attention to these more ancient versions of the liturgy because I think they help us to see better what is really going on in that sacramental moment that is at the very heart of our celebration of the Divine Liturgy. The point is that when the priest says, "Let us lift up our hearts," this is not just a pious way of saying: "Cheer up." And when the people say, "We lift them up to the Lord," we are not just saying, "We're going to focus on God for a while."

Instead, the priest says, "Let us lift up our hearts," and the people are saying, "Our hearts are *already* lifted up. There they are; there are our hearts, up there with God."

My brothers and sisters, today we celebrate the great feast of the Ascension of our Lord Jesus Christ. This is indeed the feast of the lifting up of our hearts. Today, our Lord Jesus Christ is lifted up in glory to the right hand of the Father, and he lifts up our nature with him, and he lifts up our hearts with him. So now our hearts are no longer on earth, but they have been lifted up with the Lord on high, so we can look up toward the highest heavens and say, "There are our hearts, up on high; there they are with God."

When we celebrate this feast, in faith and sincerity, the grace that we receive can truly change our lives. This grace, in fact, can entirely change the direction of our lives and turn our lives upside down—or, rather, downside up. Sometimes, we can think piously of our lives as a journey from earth to heaven. And that is true. But, in fact, this is not the deepest mystery of the Christian life. A much deeper mystery, which we celebrate today, is that in Christ our lives are a journey from heaven back to earth and then back once again, for a final time, to heaven. In other words, our Christian lives are not a one-way ticket to heaven. Rather, Christ has purchased for us a return ticket, from heaven to earth and back to heaven. Christ is already in heaven; he is already seated at the right hand of the Father in the fullness of glory. And our hearts are already with him there. But while our hearts are anchored with him there, in his glory, at the right hand of the Father, we return to the earth—just like the apostles returned to Galilee after they witnessed the ascension of the Lord—but our hearts remain in heaven. We return to the earth so that we may join what remains of the earth to our hearts that remain in heaven, at the right hand of the Father.

So, my brothers and sisters, on this wonderful feast of the Ascension of our Lord, let us lift up our hearts. Or, rather, let us acknowledge that our hearts have already been lifted up to the Lord through the ascension of our

Lord Jesus Christ. When our hearts are troubled and grieved by the darkness and sin and death of this world, let us remember that our hearts no longer belong to this world. Let us never allow our hearts to be held captive by the powers and dominions and deceitful pleasures and miseries of this world. Let us ascend with the one who *Ps. 68:18* made captivity captive and gave gifts to human beings, *Eph. 4:8* above all the gift of the Holy Spirit by which the love of God is poured into our hearts.

Let us lift up our hearts now as we approach the holy table, where the one who has ascended descends once again to nourish us with his own body and blood—the power of his life and death—so that we may ascend with him and re-find our hearts with him at the right hand of the Father. As we partake of this ascension meal, let us also be gladdened by the Lord's promise of a new out-pouring of the Holy Spirit. And while we celebrate this great feast of the Ascension of our Lord and await the celebration of the great feast of Pentecost, let us give un-ceasing thanks for the super-abounding mercies of our great God and Father, who grants us grace upon grace, and guides us from glory to greater glory, who lifts up our hearts in the ascension of his only begotten Son and fills them with his life and love in the outpouring of his Spirit. May our hearts always abound in praise and thanksgiving to this great and glorious and only true God: the Father, the Son, and the Holy Spirit, now and always and forever and ever. Amen.

PENTECOST

Unwrap the Gift
of the Spirit

Ephesians 5:8–19; Matthew 18:10–20

Brothers and sisters who are dearly beloved in Christ Jesus our Lord:

On this great feast of Pentecost that we celebrate today, God offers us the gift that surpasses and includes every other good gift, the gift of his very life and breath, the gift of his holiness and his Spirit, the gift of his Holy Spirit. At the beginning of every Divine Liturgy, the priest invokes the gift of the Holy Spirit by praying:

> Heavenly King, Consoler, Spirit of Truth, who are everywhere present and filling all things, the treasury of blessings and the Giver of Life, come and dwell in us, cleanse us of all stain and save our souls, O Good One.

The Holy Spirit is called Consoler and Comforter, because he consoles and comforts us with the love of God that is poured out in our hearts, as St. Paul tells us. He is *Rom. 5:5*
the Spirit of Truth because he guides us into the deepest *John 16:13*

truth of the inner life of God himself. The Spirit is the treasury of blessings in whom every blessing of God is given to us and through whom we learn to treasure and delight in all of God's blessings. When the Spirit dwells in us, we are cleansed from all stain and sanctified with God's own life and adorned with all the beauty and power of God's holiness.

We can go on and on reciting all the blessings and gifts that we are granted in the Holy Spirit, who was poured out on the church on the day of Pentecost, and which the Father wishes to pour out on us today on this day of Pentecost. Indeed, this is a glorious occasion, my brothers and sisters. What can be more glorious than the Holy Spirit in whom all of God's glory is communicated to us?

And yet, glorious as this feast is, it is also maybe a little bit awkward for us. It is awkward because we are afraid and even reluctant to receive this gift. There are some streams of Christian tradition that demand gifts from God and prescribe to God exactly what they want and how they want it. They demand that God demonstrate his power and love by giving them money or success or healing from diseases, and so on. My guess is that most of us in this church are not inclined to that kind of temptation. Instead, in the traditions that we belong to—the Catholic and Orthodox traditions—we often struggle with a different temptation: the temptation of being piously modest in our expectations from God. We don't expect too much and we think it is pious not to put God to the test by expecting too much. We are like the kind of person who, when you ask them how they want to celebrate their birthday or a special occasion and what kind of present they want, they always say: "I don't need anything, thank you."

Even more, sometimes we're like a person who, even when you give them a present and it's all wrapped up in front of them, they refuse to unwrap it.

"Why don't you unwrap this present?"

"Well, I don't want to presume that there's something underneath the wrapping. I'm grateful that you gave me this box with nice wrapping all around it as an expression of your care. But I don't need to actually open it as if I really expect something to be inside."

Now, wouldn't that be ridiculous? But isn't that often how we are when God offers us his greatest gifts on the most solemn and glorious feasts of the liturgical year? Think about it. What do you expect today, on this feast of Pentecost, this feast of the gift of the Holy Spirit? You like the wrapping. You love the liturgy and the singing and the talk about how wonderful the Holy Spirit is. Okay, nice wrapping. But are you going to unwrap this gift and see what's inside for *you*? Or, are you just going to admire the wrapping and feel pious because you don't want to presume that there's anything actually inside the wrapping?

When the prophet Isaiah was instructed to announce to the king of Israel, Ahaz, that God himself would come to dwell with us for our salvation, the prophet said to Ahaz: "Ask a sign of the Lord your God; let it be as deep as the underworld or as high as heaven." But Ahaz said, "I will not ask and I will not put the Lord to the test." Then Isaiah said, "Hear, then, O house of David! Is it too little for you to weary mortals, that you weary my God also? Therefore, the Lord himself will give you a sign. Look, *Isa. 7:11–14* the young woman is with child and will bear a son and he shall be called Emmanuel."

My brothers and sisters, could it be that we are like King Ahaz, who does not want to ask and put the Lord to the test, but in fact is making God weary by refusing to accept the sign that God wants to give him? Today, our heavenly Father wants to pour out his Spirit upon us in immeasurable abundance. This was why he sent his Son, as Emmanuel, to live among us and to die for us, so that we can have the gift of the Spirit, the gift of the mutual delight of the Father and the Son in the communion of their Holy Spirit.

Today, God wants us to receive this gift with eagerness and gratitude. And he tells us to ask for a sign that we have indeed received this gift: "Ask a sign of the Lord your God; let it be as deep as the underworld or high as heaven." So what shall we say? Shall we say: "I will not ask and I will not put the Lord to the test"? But what if this attitude is as wearisome to God as it is to mortals, when someone is unable and unwilling to receive the gift that you want to give them?

So, then, what sign should we ask for? We should definitely ask for a sign, I think. Should we ask for money and success and miraculous healings? I suppose that we *can*, on condition that we add that we are only asking for these things to the extent that they can contribute to our salvation, to what "is good for our souls and bodies," as we pray in the litany. But the best sign to ask for on this glorious feast of the outpouring of the Holy Spirit is the sign of the first beatitude: "Blessed are the poor in spirit; *Luke 6:20* for theirs is the kingdom of heaven." The authentic and failsafe sign that we have received the Holy Spirit is that we become poor in spirit.

What does it mean to be poor in spirit? Poverty of spirit is both similar and dissimilar to material poverty. The person who is materially poor does not rely on his own wealth, but goes around begging for money. He lives through the wealth of others, not his own wealth. In a similar way, the person who is poor in spirit does not rely on his own spirit but goes around begging for God's Spirit, and lives through the riches of God's Spirit. On the other hand, the person who is materially poor cannot always be confident that others will share their wealth with him. But the person who is poor in spirit can always be confident that God will give him his Holy Spirit in abundance and without measure: "Blessed are the poor in spirit, for theirs is the kingdom of God." Blessed are those who are filled *Luke 6:20* with the Holy Spirit, and the sign that they are filled with the Holy Spirit is that they become poor in spirit, always living not according to the flesh and not according to the promptings of their own spirit, but according to God's *Gal. 5:16* Holy Spirit.

So, my brothers and sisters, I invite you today to ask for this sign, which is as deep as the underworld and as high as heaven. To be poor in spirit is to descend into the underworld of our emptiness and sinfulness and recognize our desperate need to be uplifted and sanctified by God's Holy Spirit. To be poor in spirit is to be raised to the greatest heights of the heaven of God's glorious life through our communion in God's Holy Spirit.

The Lord told us: "Ask and it will be given to you. . . . Is there anyone among you who, if your child asks for bread or a fish, will give him a snake . . . ? If you, then, who are evil, know how to give good gifts to your children, how much more will the heavenly Father give the Holy Spirit to those who ask him?" Let us now approach the holy *Luke 11:10–13* table and boldly ask for everything that the Lord wishes to give us: the body and blood of his Son and a new and powerful outpouring of his Holy Spirit. If we earnestly ask for these great gifts, we are already poor in spirit, we are already receiving the gift of the Holy Spirit. But the Lord wants us to keep asking, both for the gift of the Holy Spirit and the sign that we have received this gift, which is our being poor in spirit. Let us rejoice in this sign and exult in this gift, through which we become true citizens of the blessed kingdom of the Father, the Son, and the Holy Spirit. Amen.

THE DIFFERENCE
THE SPIRIT MAKES

Acts 2:1–11; John 7:37–52; 8:12

Brothers and sisters who are dearly beloved in Christ Jesus our Lord:

In the Byzantine tradition, we typically begin all our prayers, including the Divine Liturgy, with this prayer to the Holy Spirit:

> Heavenly King, Consoler, Spirit of Truth, who are everywhere present and filling all things, the treasury of blessings and the Giver of Life, come and dwell in us, cleanse us of all stain and save our souls, O Good One.

But it is also traditional in the Byzantine tradition to repress that prayer from Easter to Pentecost. From Easter to the feast of the Ascension, it is replaced with the troparion of Easter: "Christ is risen from the dead, trampling down death by death, and on those in the tomb, bestowing life."

Before this year, the practice of repressing the opening prayer to the Holy Spirit had not made much of an impression on me. But this Easter season I found it quite difficult—though one benefit was that it led me to repent of the way I had always looked down on the Western practice of repressing the "Alleluias" during Lent. It had seemed to me that repressing the "Alleluias" was like pretending that we didn't know that Christ is risen and I appreciated the way that the Byzantine liturgy reminded us to rejoice in the resurrection even during Lent. But this year I found myself wondering about what amounted to a similar practice in the Byzantine tradition during the Easter season. What was the point of repressing the prayer to the Holy Spirit after Easter, as if we were pretending that the Holy Spirit had not already been given to us—as if it was still the case, as we read in our gospel today, that "as yet there *John 7:39* was no Spirit, because Jesus was not yet glorified"? We know that Jesus has been glorified and has poured out his Spirit on us in the sacrament of chrismation, so why do we have to repress this prayer to the Holy Spirit in preparation for celebrating this feast of Pentecost?

But then I reminded myself that, of course, we are not prohibited from praying to the Holy Spirit. Nevertheless, the comfort of a ready-made prayer to the Spirit is taken away from us during this period precisely so that we do not fall into the complacency of just presuming that we "have" the Spirit, and so that we can really strive for the Spirit in our own words—as need be—and in the silence of our hearts, and of course, with the Holy Spirit himself *Rom. 8:26* interceding for us with sighs too deep for words.

I also came to experience that moment when I was about to recite the prayer to the Holy Spirit and had to stop myself and ask for the Spirit on my own, as it were, as very valuable in drawing me into the mystery of what is at stake when we ask for the Holy Spirit. I would like to share with you two lessons that I learned, two graces that I felt I received by following this practice.

In the first place, in a paradoxical way, it helped me to appreciate more deeply the distinctive role of the Spirit precisely in drawing us into the power of the resurrection of Christ. When I was praying the Easter troparion, "Christ is risen from the dead . . . ," without having said the customary prayer to the Holy Spirit, I felt disconnected, at least for a moment, from the resurrection of Christ. That very experience of disconnection impressed on me how the Holy Spirit is the One who connects us to the resurrection of Christ. If Christ just rose from the dead, without sending us the Holy Spirit, then his resurrection would belong just to him. We could marvel at the fact that Christ rose from the dead, we can admire it, but we would be just admiring and marveling at something that happened to him, not something that happens to us.

But because Christ sent us the Holy Spirit, everything that happened to him happens to us. This work of the Spirit reveals a central feature of his personal identity, which is to take what belongs to each and make it the common property of all. That is what the Spirit does even within the Holy Trinity. The Spirit is the One in whom the Father and the Son pour out the communion of their love, so that the uniqueness of the Father and the uniqueness of the Son are exchanged and shared in their common love. The Spirit works and manifests himself in a similar way in the church, distributing gifts to each that are meant to be shared by all. The Spirit grants gifts to "each one individually just as the Spirit chooses," but "to each is given the manifestation of the Spirit for the common good." For this reason, too, the effect of the Spirit's descent upon the apostles was to make them "of one heart and soul, and no

1 Cor. 12:11

1 Cor. 12:7

one claimed private ownership of any possessions, but ev-

Acts 4:32 erything they owned was held in common." For all these reasons, we speak of the Holy Spirit as the One who creates communion and fellowship, as when the priest gives the blessing in the liturgy: "The grace of our Lord Jesus Christ, the love of God the Father, and the *communion* of the Holy Spirit be with all of you." It is the Holy Spirit who enables us to have communion in the grace of our Lord Jesus Christ and in the love of God the Father.

And so, it is the Spirit who makes all the power of Christ's resurrection belong to us, as St. Paul tells us:

> If the Spirit of him who raised Jesus from the dead dwells in you, he who raised Jesus from the dead will
> *Rom. 8:11* give life to your mortal bodies also through the Spirit that dwells in you.

So, when we pray the "Christ is risen," while repressing the prayer to the Holy Spirit, this helps us to recognize, for just a brief moment, the distance and disconnection between Christ's resurrection and us, as long as the Holy Spirit is not involved. But, of course, the Holy Spirit is involved, and so we are impelled by the Spirit to call on the Spirit to dwell in us and to bridge that distance and banish that disconnection between the risen Lord and us. To the exact extent that the Holy Spirit dwells in us, he makes everything that belongs to Christ belong to us, even his divine sonship. If Christ had not sent us the Holy Spirit, he alone would be the only begotten Son of God. But because he has received the Holy Spirit in his humanity on our behalf and has sent us the Spirit, the only begotten Son of God has become "the firstborn of many" children
Rom. 8:29 of God. His divine sonship now belongs to us, as St. Paul also teaches us:

When we cry, "Abba, Father," it is that same Spirit bearing witness with our spirit that we are children of God,
and if children, then heirs, heirs of God and joint heirs
with Christ—if, in fact, we suffer with him so that we
may also be glorified with him.

Rom. 8:15–17

It is the Holy Spirit who grants us fellowship and communion with Christ's saving suffering and with Christ's
glorification and makes everything that belongs to him as
the only begotten Son our inheritance as adopted children
of God.

There was a second lesson I learned, and another
grace that I received, while following the practice of repressing the ready-made prayer to the Holy Spirit. In that
brief moment when I had to stop myself from saying that
prayer, I initially felt deprived of the consolation of the
Holy Spirit. I had associated the consolation of the Spirit
so much with that specific prayer to the Holy Spirit as
"Consoler and Spirit of Truth." But then I began to experience that momentary desolation as a revelation of how
I was repressing the Holy Spirit elsewhere in my life.

The thought occurred to me that there was an analogy
to be drawn here with the way people who take breathing lessons—whether for health reasons or as part of
voice training, for example—are taught to be attentive
to how they are repressing their natural breathing. That
momentary repression of the prayer to the Holy Spirit
revealed to me the spiritual pain and desolation of repressing the Spirit, of "stifling the Spirit," which I do all
the time. St. Paul teaches us that we stifle and repress the
Spirit whenever we walk according to the flesh—that is,
whenever we are ruled by the agenda of our merely natural needs and desires: "For those who live according to the
flesh set their minds on the things of the flesh, but those

1 Thess. 5:19

Rom. 8:5

Gal. 5:25

1 Pet. 4:2

John 7:37

John 7:37–38

Gal. 5:22

who live according to the Spirit set their minds on the things of the Spirit." But if we live by the Spirit, we need to walk according to the Spirit; we need to let the Spirit guide us in the path of growing into the divine sonship of Christ; we need to live "no longer by human desires but by the will of God." When the Spirit reveals to us how much we stifle and repress the Spirit, our thirst for the Spirit becomes keener and more desperate. And then we can respond more eagerly to the words of our Lord: "Let anyone who is thirsty come to me, and let the one who believes in me drink." The Holy Spirit is poured out of the heart of the risen Lord like living waters, and when he shares this Spirit with us, the Spirit also flows out of our hearts and into all the world.

This is the invitation and the promise that the Lord extends to us today, on this great feast of Pentecost. Today, our risen Lord, Jesus Christ, is standing in our midst at this liturgy and breathing the Spirit into us and saying to each one of us, "Receive the Holy Spirit. Receive all the fruits of sharing in my divine sonship: my love, my joy, my peace, my patience, my kindness, my generosity, my faithfulness, my gentleness, my integrity." Today the Holy Spirit himself liberates us from our repression of his power and his glory in us. Today, we should not feel any distance or disconnection from the resurrection and glorification of our Lord Jesus Christ. Through the grace of the Holy Spirit, Christ's resurrection and his glorification belong entirely to us. We can breathe in the new life of his resurrection and the fragrance of his glorification in our every breath through the Holy Spirit that he pours out on us. Today, after striving on our own to call on the Holy Spirit, we have the comfort of the prayer that the church gives us to assure us of the presence and power of the Holy Spirit in our midst:

Heavenly King, Consoler, Spirit of Truth, who are everywhere present and filling all things, the treasury of
blessings and the Giver of Life, come and dwell in us,
cleanse us of all stain and save our souls, O Good One.

Let us now approach the holy table of the Eucharist
so that we may receive the gift of the Holy Spirit that is
granted to us through the body and blood of our risen
Lord. We know that it is certainly not merely the material flesh of Christ that we receive in the holy Eucharist
but the Spirit that animated and sanctified and divinized
his body and blood. When we eat the body of Christ and
drink the blood of Christ, we are filled with the Spirit of
Christ. May we be filled to overflowing with that Spirit
whom the Father grants us without measure, so that we   *John 3:34*
may partake ever more fully of the grace of our Lord Jesus
Christ, and the love of God the Father, and the communion of the Holy Spirit. Amen.

TRANSFIGURATION

The Glory of Christ
in His and Our Suffering

2 Peter 1:10–19; Matthew 17:1–9

My brothers and sisters who are dearly beloved in Christ Jesus our Lord:

Today is a great feast for us, the feast of the glory of God shining in the face of our Lord Jesus Christ, the feast in which we become eyewitnesses of this glory, the glory of God's only begotten Son, who reflects even in his humanity the full radiance of the Father's glory. To- *Heb. 1:3* day, we also receive a vision of our future glory, when our humanity will be transfigured into the likeness of Christ's divine humanity.

As often happens with even the greatest of God's gifts, this feast can catch us by surprise. It comes to us in the unassuming style of God's wonderful humility, and it is easy for us to just pass by it without making a big deal about it—or, to just let it be a little pious distraction and then we move on with our lives as before. It is especially easy to be inattentive to the power of this great feast of the Transfiguration of our Lord because it seems to come out

231

of nowhere. There is no big liturgical build-up, there is no secular buy-in like we have with Christmas and Easter. All of a sudden, it seems, out of nowhere, we have the glory of Christ: What are we supposed to do with that?

I think that a key part of the answer to this question is that today we celebrate not just the glory of Christ in an abstract way, but the glory of Christ that is manifested in our everyday lives, and especially in our suffering. This key is provided for us in the liturgical placement of this feast exactly forty days before the Feast of the Exaltation of the Holy Cross on September 14. This liturgical logic reflects the logic of the Scriptures, in which the transfiguration accounts in all three synoptic gospels immediately follow Jesus's announcement to his disciples that he will suffer and die and be raised on the third day. Peter re-*Matt. 16:22* sponds by saying, "God forbid that this should happen *and par.* to you, Lord." And, of course, Jesus rebukes him strongly *Matt. 16:23* by saying, "Get behind me, Satan." And then we have the *and par.* transfiguration.

Through the juxtaposition of Jesus's rebuke of Peter and his transfiguration, the Gospels present us with two conflicting visions of the glory of our Lord Jesus Christ. One is the vision of Peter, which wants Jesus to reflect God's glory by avoiding shame and suffering. And Jesus says bluntly: that vision of God's glory comes from Satan. But then Jesus grants Peter and James and John a true and genuine and resplendent vision of his true glory, a glory that does not run away from suffering but a glory that is also not diminished by suffering—a glory that gives us the power to persevere and even rejoice in the midst of this suffering. This is exactly the interpretation that we find in the kontakion* for our feast today:

---

* A "kontakion," like a "troparion," is a short liturgical hymn.

On the mountain you were transfigured, O Christ our God, and your disciples saw as much of your glory as they could hold, so that when they should see you crucified they would know that you suffer willingly and would proclaim to the world that you are verily the Splendor of the Father.*

My brothers and sisters, we tend to think of glory and happiness and perfection as something that we are supposed to experience at the end of our lives, after we have suffered, after we have paid the price of admission to this glory by our suffering. But the Christian vision of reality is different. It is true that we await the fullness of the constant and perfect vision of God's glory at the end of history, after the second coming of our Lord. But it has never been God's way to simply withhold his glory until the very end. According to the Christian revelation, it has always been God's way to give us his glory, right at the beginning, and constantly throughout our lives. And it has always been the Christian revelation that we need the vision of God's glory in order to just survive from day to day. The vision of God's glory is not just the prize at the end of the way of salvation; the vision of God's glory is what makes it possible for us to even start on the way of salvation and to persevere in this way.

A great witness to this truth is Moses, who appeared with Elijah during the transfiguration of our Lord. Moses had been promised by God that he would lead the people of Israel out of slavery and oppression in Egypt into a land of their own, where they could live in peace as God's chosen people. But Moses is inspired to realize that this liber-

---

* *August Menaion*, Service Books of the Byzantine Churches (Boston, MA: Sophia Press, 2010), 86.

ation cannot happen merely with God's help and without God's personal and glorious accompaniment. Moses realizes that the liberation of God's people cannot be accomplished only by God's powerful deeds, like the plagues and the parting of the Red Sea. These are helpful, but that's not really how the fullness of salvation comes about. Moses realizes that the fullness of salvation is accomplished only when God himself is present in all his glory. And so Moses says to the Lord: "'If your presence will not go with us, do not carry us from here. For how shall it be known that I have found favor in your sight, I and your people, unless you go with us?' . . . Then the Lord said to Moses, 'I will do the very thing that you have asked: for you have found favor in my sight, and I know you by name.' Moses said, 'Show me your glory, I pray.' And the Lord said, 'I will make all my goodness pass before you, and will proclaim before you the name, the LORD, and I will be gracious to

Exod. 33:15–23   whom I will be gracious and will show mercy to whom I will show mercy. But . . . you cannot see my face; for no one shall see me and live . . . you shall see my back; but my face shall not be seen.'"

My brothers and sisters, when Moses appeared at the transfiguration of the Lord, he did see God's glory shining in the face of Christ, which shone more brightly than the sun. His presence at the transfiguration of our Lord was the fulfillment of the prayer that he made right at the start of the history of our redemption: "Show me your glory, I pray." But Moses still leads the way for us in encountering the glory of God in Christ because he teaches us that above all we need not just God's help but the vision of God's glory: "Show me your glory, I pray." And without this vision, we cannot go on, we cannot go anywhere: "If your presence will not go with us, do not carry us from here."

The inspired psalmist reveals the same truth to us when he prays: "Restore us, O God. Let your face shine on us." This is also our prayer today. Today, the ground of our celebration and our joy is not a matter of indulging in a little pious distraction from the burdens of our daily lives and the misery of the news cycle that daily reveals the brutality and viciousness of our fallen humanity. Today, we gather as a people in desperate need of salvation, of restoration, knowing that our restoration can only begin with the vision of God's glory: "Restore us, O God. Let your face shine on us."   *Ps. 80:3*

So, my brothers and sisters, let us mystically and sacramentally go up the mountain with Peter, James, and John and with Moses and Elijah. Let us not attempt to go up this mountain of divine encounter with the false expectation that God's glory will shield us from all suffering. Such an expectation, as our Lord told Peter, does not come from the Holy Spirit but from Satan. Let us rather go up with the inspired knowledge that God's glory always goes before us in the midst of our sufferings, like a cloud by day and a pillar of fire by night, always present to us in the face of Christ that gazes upon us both day and night. It is the vision of this glory that will enable us always to rejoice even in the midst of our personal suffering and the suffering of this broken and anguished world.

Let us now eat and drink this glory and become glorified while glorifying in all things the only true and almighty and all-loving God, the Father, the Son, and the Holy Spirit.

DORMITION

Mary, Exemplar of the Glory of Our Humanity

Philippians 2:5–11; Luke 10:38–42; 11:27–28

My brothers and sisters who are dearly beloved in Jesus Christ our Lord:

Today we give great thanks to God our Father for gathering us together—for the first time in too long a time—to partake of the sacred body and blood of his only begotten Son and to be filled with his life-giving and God-giving Spirit.* We especially give thanks today that our loving God has arranged in his wonderful providence to gather us together again in time for us to celebrate together the great feast of the Dormition of the Mother of God, the patroness of our community.

What a wonderful and deep consolation it is for us to celebrate this great feast of our Lady at a time when we are in such great and desperate need of her motherly intercession and of the plentiful grace that flows through her, through the power and mercy of her son, our Lord Jesus Christ.

---

* This homily was preached on August 14, 2020, after a period of Covid shutdown.

In celebrating this beautiful feast in this present time of great affliction, we are celebrating the glory of the human race at a time when this glory is otherwise very hard to see, at a time when it is very hard to believe that there is anything at all glorious about being human. This pandemic has humiliated our pride and shown us how suddenly useless all our intelligence can be in the face of a tiny microbe. It has exposed all the deep-rooted structural sins and vices of our society to the point where it seems that we can justly apply to ourselves the judgment of the prophet Isaiah:

> The whole head is sick,
> and the whole heart faint.
> From the sole of the foot even to the head,
> there is no soundness in it,
> but bruises and sores and bleeding wounds;
> they have not been drained or bound up,
> or softened with oil.
> Your country lies desolate.

Isa. 1:5–7

But, today, in the midst of this desolation, in the midst of all this evidence of the susceptibility of our race to physical and moral and spiritual sickness, we have the counterevidence of the young woman from Nazareth who became the Mother of God. We have the counterevidence of the human being whose body and soul became—and will forever be—the sacred temple of the living God. In her we see the fulfillment of God's great plan for glorifying the human race, which St. Paul speaks about when he says: "We know all things work together for good, for those who love God, who are called according to his purpose. For those whom he foreknew, he also predestined

to be conformed to the image of his Son. . . . And those
whom he predestined, he also called; and those whom   *Rom. 8:28–30*
he called, he also justified; and those whom he justified,
he also glorified."

My brothers and sisters, despite all the devastation we
are now experiencing, God's plan is for us to be glorified
in him, to be filled with his glory. This is the destiny that
God has in store for us, which has already been fulfilled
in Mary, a glorious destiny that we can already contemplate and celebrate by looking to her and rejoicing in the
fullness of her grace.

But Mary does not just show us the end of the path of
glory that God has planned for us; she also shows us the
way to this glory and accompanies us at every step of that
way. She is not only the one who is herself full of grace but
also the one who is always eager to share the fullness of her
grace with us. She is always willing to lead us in the path
of letting our bodies be dwelling places for the Lord and
giving over the whole of our minds and wills to the contemplation of Jesus Christ and to obedience to his will.

It is intriguing that, in the Byzantine liturgy, the gospel
for this feast day does not really focus on Mary herself.
Mary does not actually appear or say anything in the gospel for this feast. Our gospel reading first speaks of a different Mary, not the mother of Jesus but the sister of Martha,
who sat at the Lord's feet and listened to his word. And,
then, when a woman in the crowd tries to compliment
Jesus's mother, saying, "Blessed is the womb that bore you
and the breasts that nursed you," Jesus seems to deflect the
compliment by saying, "Blessed rather are those who hear   *Luke 11:27–28*
the word of God and obey it."

What today's gospel wants to tell us, in this round-
about way, is that what is most wonderful about Mary is

not that she merely physically gave birth to the incarnate God, which is a wonderful grace that no one else can ever share in. But what is an even more wonderful grace is that Mary is the one who excelled more than any other human being in sitting at the Lord's feet and listening to his Word, and in hearing the Word of God and obeying it. And this grace we can all share in, through her powerful and constant intercession, and sharing in this grace is our way to glory.

My brothers and sisters, if we ask ourselves how we can advance on this way of glory in our present circumstances, as our world is overshadowed by the dark cloud of this pandemic, the answer is surely not that we should merely hope and pray for things to go back to normal, to the way they were before. To hope only for things to go back to normal is like the pining of the Israelites in the wilderness for the cucumbers and melons and leeks of

Num. 11:5 Egypt. This is not the model we should follow. And I say this to you as someone who grew up in Egypt and has firsthand experience of just how tasty Egyptian cucumbers and melons can be.

Of course, we should pray for an end to the pandemic and to the terrible economic and social devastation it has caused and exposed. But our hope is for much greater things than just to return to the way things were before. Let the rest of the world pine away for the cucumbers and melons and leeks of a bygone and corrupt normalcy. We have another agenda and another path to travel. We pine only for the fullness of the kingdom of God and the final liberation of all creation from bondage to decay and for

Rom. 8:21 the freedom of the glory of the children of God, which Mary, our mother of grace and the mother of our Lord, has already attained.

On this great feast day, we must hold fast to our faith that these death pangs "of the present form of this world that is passing away" can be transformed by God's grace into the birth pangs of a new world, a new heaven and a new earth, in which all of creation will be bathed in the infinite splendor of God's glory. We must remind ourselves constantly that God does not let any evil happen without a plan to make greater good come out of it. It is up to us to let this greater good come into the world through us. This will only happen if we make use of this pandemic to resolve to become better Christians after this pandemic than we were before it, more conformed to the image of Christ, more filled with the Spirit, less servile to the powers of sin and death, more dedicated to the glorious servanthood of the freedom of the children of God.

1 Cor. 7:31

Rom. 8:22

Today we ask her who is full of grace to intercede for us to receive all these graces, which she is so eager to grant us, all these graces that will enable us to live through this pandemic in such a way as to let the old world of corruption die in us and to let the new world bathed in God's glory to rise up in us.

To nourish us on the path of this grace, we do not look to the cucumbers and melons of Egypt but only to the true bread from heaven, the body and blood of our Lord Jesus Christ. In him, everything that leads to physical and spiritual death has been put to death; in him, everything that brings eternal life and everlasting glory is freely granted to us. Let us now gratefully partake of this body and blood. Let us digest this spiritual food and drink not only through our physical organs, but above all by sitting at the Lord's feet and listening to his words and obeying his word, with all our hearts and all our minds and all our strength.

John 6:32

Mark 12:30

May she who was full of the grace of perfect obedience lead us to the fullness of glory that she has already
attained and which she always desires to share with us,
through the grace of her son, our Lord Jesus Christ, and
the love of God the Father, and the communion of the
Holy Spirit. Amen.

BECOMING MOTHERS OF GOD

Philippians 2:5–11; Luke 10:38–42; 11:27–28

Brothers and sisters who are dearly beloved in Christ Jesus our Lord:

Today our souls magnify the Lord and our spirits rejoice in God our Savior as we celebrate the Dormition and assumption into heavenly glory of the holy Mother of God. We magnify the Lord and we rejoice in God our Savior because he looked with favor on the lowliness of his servant, whom he has made into his mother, and has lifted her up higher than every principality and power and granted her more honor than the cherubim and more glory than the seraphim, this poor woman from Nazareth whom God chose to crown as queen of heaven and earth.

My brothers and sisters, it has been rightly said that grace builds on nature. The glorious acts of God's economy of grace do not destroy the wondrous works of his creation but manifest even more clearly the wonders of his creation. Nowhere is that more evident and more joyful than in the way the beautiful mystery of human motherhood is taken up into the glorious mystery of Mary's motherhood of God.

What a great and beautiful mystery it is that every human being has a mother. Even if some of us here no longer have mothers living on this earth—mothers who have fallen asleep in the Lord, as Mary herself did—and even if it sometimes happens that a child is separated from its biological mother immediately after birth for some reason or other—it is nevertheless always true that every human being has a mother. Which means that every human being enters the world co-bodied in the body of another human being—his or her mother. The body of every human being begins its existence within the body of his or her mother. The mother makes space in her body for her child; she shares her body and her blood and her very life with the child. In this way, every human being enters the world enveloped by the radical hospitality of his or her mother. That is how we are initiated, from the moment of our conception, into the mystery of God's hospitality, mediated by the hospitality of our mothers. A mother proclaims to her child, in the most physical and tangible way, that the world is a hospitable place because she herself becomes that hospitable place through which we enter the world.

Great and wonderful as is this mystery of *human* motherhood, how infinitely greater and more unutterably wonderful still is the mystery that *God* chose to come into the world by being born of a human mother. Being God, he didn't have to do this. He could have become human without becoming a baby in the womb of his mother. But God himself chose to enter the world through the hospitality of a human mother. He chose to enter the world co-bodied in the body of Mary and to begin his human life by sharing her body and her blood and her very life.

He chose to enter the world by depending on her for his physical and emotional nourishment, feeding at her breast, gazing into her eyes, seeking and responding to her smile. He chose to embrace this dependence on his mother as the first stage of the mystery of his self-emptying, which we read about in the epistle reading for today. Though he was in the form of God, he emptied himself and took on the form of a servant — first of all, by taking on the form of a helpless human child, utterly dependent on his mother.

The Gospels give us unmistakable hints that our Lord continued to embrace this natural human relationship with his mother throughout his life, while also initiating her ever deeper into the mystery of his divine sonship and mission. As a child, he calms his mother's anxiety when she finds him in the temple after thinking that he was lost and explains to her that he must always be occupied with his heavenly Father's business. At the wedding in Cana, he banters with his mother and finally gives in to her intercession on behalf of the married couple who have run out of wine. At the foot of the cross, he asks his mother to extend her motherly hospitality to his beloved disciple ("Woman, behold your son") and he invites his disciple to accept Mary as his own mother: "Behold, your mother."

And even though the Gospels do not tell us anything about Mary's death, it is both reasonable in itself and in keeping with scriptural logic to assume that Mary died, like every other human being, including her son, and that when she died our Lord crowned her with glory and honor and received her soul into his embrace, just like she received his body into her bodily embrace when he came into the world. After accepting her motherly hospitality on earth, he extended to her his divine hospitality in heaven.

Sometimes, we hear of someone who suddenly becomes rich—someone who signs a big contract to play professional basketball, for example—and the first thing they do is buy their mom a big house. So, Jesus does something like that, though on a rather bigger scale. Is it not fitting that he who said, "In my Father's house, there are many dwellings. . . . I go to prepare a place for you . . . so *John 14:2–3* that where I am, there you may be also" did not waste any time in preparing a preeminent dwelling for his own mother, so that she may dwell with him, where he is, in the fullness of his glory?

My brothers and sisters, among all the beautiful and glorious aspects of this joyous feast that we celebrate today, let us now consider two wonderful graces that are offered to each of us as we celebrate this holy day.

First, we are offered the grace of accepting anew the offer of Mary's motherly hospitality. Today, our Lord says to each one of us, "Behold, your mother." In these difficult and turbulent and anxious and godless times, in these times in which we are tempted to at least figuratively if not literally assume a fetal position of helplessness and fear, how great is our need of the spiritual motherhood of Mary, the Mother of God! How great is God's mercy and tenderness that even when we are reborn through the Spirit, when we become children of God, who are born *John 1:13* not of blood, nor of the will of man, but of God—even in that spiritual birth, and throughout our life in the Spirit, we still have a mother! A mother who always looks on us with tenderness, who always seeks to comfort us, and is always ready to intercede for us. A mother to whom we can run when the wine of this passing world is running out and all our joy seems depleted, who will guide us back to her son and will always intercede for us to be granted the new wine of his everlasting kingdom. Let us run to her even now and heed the call of her son: Behold, your mother.

Yet, as wonderful as is this grace of receiving the hospitality of Mary's motherhood, today we are offered a second and even more glorious grace: the grace of actually sharing in Mary's motherhood of God. The glory of Mary's role in the mystery of our salvation is not only that she is our mother in Christ, but even more, that she intercedes for us and helps us to become ourselves mothers *of* Christ and mothers of God. Shocking as that may sound, that seems to be exactly the point of our reading of the particular gospel passage that we read for today's feast. On this feast of the glorification of Mary, the mother of God and the mother of Christ, we read that a woman said to our Lord, "Blessed is the womb that bore you and the breasts that nursed you." Yet, Jesus responds: "Blessed rather are those who hear the word of God and obey it." *Luke 11:27–28* Of course, Jesus is not saying that Mary is not blessed, for she is the one who, above all others, heard the Word of God and obeyed it and embodied it in her own flesh. But our Lord is saying that Mary's blessedness does not consist only in her physical motherhood but, even more, in her spiritual motherhood, by which she gives birth to the Word of God in her every action and every word and every thought.

None of us can duplicate Mary's physical motherhood of Christ but we can all share in her spiritual motherhood of Christ. When we hear the Word of God and obey it and put it into action, we also give birth to God in our flesh; we also provide hospitality to God and nurture his presence and become his mother. And that is why Jesus says elsewhere, in the Gospel of Matthew, "'Who is my mother and my brothers?' And pointing to his disciples he said, 'Here are my mother and my brothers. Whoever *Matt. 12:48–49* does the will of my Father in heaven is my brother and sister *and mother.*"

So, my brothers and sisters, as we approach the holy altar of the Lord to enjoy the gifts of his hospitality, let us partake of the nourishment that will enable us to be brothers and sisters and even *mothers* of our Lord. In his great generosity, he extends to us his abundant hospitality; in his great humility, he asks us to extend hospitality to him. He fills the hungry with good things, even his own body and blood, and he longs to be embodied in our bodies and mingled with our blood. He is our heavenly Father who wants each of us to be his mother. What great mysteries these are, my brothers and sisters, at which even the angels in heaven who celebrate this divine liturgy with us are amazed.

In communion with these angels and all the heavenly hosts, and in the company of the one who is more honorable and glorious than all of them, our most highly blessed and glorious lady, the Mother of God and ever-virgin Mary, let us indeed magnify the Lord and rejoice in God our Savior—the only true and saving and glorious God, Father, Son, and Holy Spirit, now and forever. Amen.

ELECTION HOMILY

Voting in Christ:
Evangelical Counsel
before a Federal Election

1 Corinthians 12:27–13:7; Luke 16:19–31

Brothers and sisters who are dearly beloved in Christ Jesus our Lord:

As we await the coming election, let us remember the admonition of St. Paul, in his letter to Timothy, saying: "I urge that supplications be made for everyone, for kings and all who are in high positions, so that we may lead a quiet and peaceable life in all godliness and dignity." So *1 Tim. 2:2* today, we pray for those who are seeking high positions in our country, and we pray that the results of this election will further the common good and enable us to live in peace and tranquility, pursuing godliness and the dignity of all people. As we make this prayer, we also give thanks

---

This sermon was preached on November 1, 2020. Admittedly, the proximity of a federal election is not in itself a liturgical feast and thus the logic of its inclusion in this volume is not self-evident. Nevertheless, I include it out of the conviction that the liturgical proclamation of the gospel must enfold and critique our political commitments.

for God's providence, which has wonderfully arranged for us the nourishment of the Word of God that especially meets our current needs and deals with the anxieties of the present hour.

What is at stake in all political questions is the basic question of how people should live together and deal with each other. Today, the Word of God lays before us two ways in which this question can be answered. One way leads to the kingdom of God and is already a foretaste and a preview of the life of the kingdom. The other way leads to perdition and brings with it the torment of social breakdown and mutual hostility that we are already experiencing in our society.

The first way is laid out before us in our first reading, from St. Paul's Letter to the Corinthians. St. Paul says to the church of Corinth, and through the Holy Spirit to the church of all times and all places, that the church is the body of Christ and each one of us is a member of that body. He had already explained this more explicitly earlier in his letter, saying: "For in the one Spirit, we were all baptized into one body—Jews or Greeks, slaves or free— *1 Cor. 12:13* and we were all made to drink of one Spirit." In today's reading, St. Paul tells us that the body of the church is animated above all by love, which is itself a gift of the Spirit. Through this love, all the members of the body together rejoice in the truth, together bear all things, together believe all things, together hope all things, together endure all things. Earlier in his letter, St. Paul had also exhorted the Corinthians to practice this communion in love when *1 Cor. 12:26* he said: "If one member suffers, all suffer together; if one member is honored, all rejoice together with it."

Now, it is true that St. Paul is here speaking specifically about the church, about those who have been baptized into

Christ and have received the gifts of the Spirit, of which love is the greatest. But it is also true that the church is the goal of all creation, and this truth was reproclaimed by the Second Vatican Council when it said that the church is "the universal sacrament of salvation."* God created human beings for this final end: that they may become members together of the one body of his only begotten Son. He sent his only begotten Son into the world for this same end: that he may take to himself a human body into which all humanity can be incorporated, and that he may break down all divisions through his death on the cross, so that there may be no separation among the members of the one body. He poured out his Holy Spirit for that very same end: that the love which binds together the Father and the Son in eternal delight may bind together all the members of Christ's body in the joy of their communion in the love of the Father and the Son.

Eph. 2:14

So, that is the first way that the Word of God lays before us today: the way that leads to the communion of all humanity in the body of Christ and in the life of the Holy Trinity. As Christians, it has been revealed to us that this is the way to which every human heart secretly aspires; this is the way that is the ultimate standard for every human society; this is the way in which we must always travel, never turning to the right or to the left, regardless of how human powers and principalities try to move us or coerce us.

There is, of course, another way, and that is the way with which we are more familiar in this fallen world. It is the way shown forth in today's gospel reading. This is the way not of communion but of isolation, in which "a great

* *Lumen Gentium* 48.

Luke 16:26   chasm has been fixed" between the rich and the poor, between the powerful and the weak, between the born and
the unborn, between white and black, between one individual and another. In this way, the goal of each individual
is simply to acquire goods for him- or herself—to dress in
purple and fine linen and to feast sumptuously every day,
disregarding anyone else who may be lying helplessly at
our gate. It was to destroy this way that the only begotten Son of God put aside the vesture of his divinity and
the feast of his eternal perfections and crossed the great
chasm between us and him and clothed us with his divinity and feasted us with his body and blood, that we may
become all together members of his body. And yet, this
second way, the way of division and mutual alienation,
still persists. Every day of our lives, we have the choice
before us of which way to take: the way of the body of
Christ or the way of gated isolation.

So now, we can ask: In setting before us these two
ways, in today's liturgy, how is the Word of God preparing
us to face the concerns and anxieties of the days ahead, as
we await the election results?

Of course, it would be out of place for me to tell you
how to vote, if you have not already voted. You must make
your own prudential judgment as to which of the available options will more readily enable our society to live
in peace and tranquility and to pursue the godliness and
dignity of God's ultimate plan for all humanity to become
members of the one body of his Christ, filled with the
Spirit of his love. But, perhaps the most important message that the Word of God wants to relay to us today is
that, as Christians, we do not stand or fall with the results
of this election, whatever these results may be. We are certainly not waiting to find out who will lead us for the next
four years; we know the one who will lead us not only for

the next few years but for all eternity, "the only King of
kings and Lord of lords," who became a servant for our   *Rev. 17:14*
sake, to raise us up to his glory. And we are certainly not
waiting for or expecting any earthly government to transform this world into the kingdom of God. This has already
been accomplished by Jesus Christ and it is our task as
Christians to share the fruits of this accomplishment with
the rest of the world. Different earthly powers can provide
different opportunities and different obstacles to our pur-
suance of this task. But the task will always be there and its
ultimate accomplishment is already assured.

So, for the next four years and for the rest of our lives,
we have our work cut out for us, regardless of the out-
come of this election and regardless of the rise and fall of
all earthly powers: to proclaim and witness to the better
way of the kingdom of Christ, the kingdom in which all
humanity is invited to become members of his one body.
Our constant task is to proclaim and witness to this better
way in the peacefulness and meekness of Christ and in the
love of the Holy Spirit, in season and out of season, by
words or in prayerful silence, with patience and kindness,
without envy or boastfulness or arrogance or rudeness,
not insisting on our own way, not being irritable or resentful because we are despised by others, never rejoicing
in wrongdoing, always rejoicing in the truth and never
acquiescing in lies; bearing all things even with those who
can't stand us, believing all things even with those who do
not share our faith, hoping all things even for the sake of
those who hope for our demise; enduring all things while   *1 Cor. 13:4–7*
interceding for those who cannot endure us.

My brothers and sisters, since we know our task and
are assured of its accomplishment in Christ, let us now
feast with him, rejoicing that he has given us this task after
he accomplished it for us, and being strengthened through

the partaking of his body and blood, that we may become
one body with him and with one another; and interceding for all those who have not yet accepted the invitation
to become members of the One in whom the fullness of
Col. 2:9   God dwells bodily. May we all become perfectly one in his
body, as he is one with the Father and the Holy Spirit, in
perfect glory and honor and in the dominion of perfect
love, now and forever. Amen.

FUNERAL HOMILIES

WHO IS DAVID BURNETT?

Wisdom of Solomon 3:1–9; Romans 8:3b–35, 37–39;
Matthew 5:1–12a

Dear family and friends:

Today, we are gathered to grieve together and to comfort one another and to be comforted by God at the passing from this earthly life of David Burnett: husband, father, grandfather, fixer-at-large, a just man who is now fully resting in the hand of God, a meek and gentle man *Wis. 3:1* who is now ready to receive his inheritance in the kingdom of God. We are gathered today to grieve together and *Matt. 5:5* to comfort each other and to be comforted by God, who is the first and ultimate source of all comfort and all consolation. But our purpose today is not only to soothe our *2 Cor. 1:3* feelings of grief. It is also, and even more importantly, to witness to the truth of the ultimate meaning and destiny of human life, and especially to witness to the truth and ultimate meaning of the unique life of David Burnett.

Last Sunday, I read a terribly sad essay in the *New York Times*. It was written by a woman whose baby had died at

---

This sermon was preached at a Roman Catholic funeral liturgy for my father-in-law.

only four months old. This woman had been a Jehovah's Witness but, before she had this baby, she had left that religion, along with all belief in the existence of a god. Her essay spoke of her anguish in coping with, in her own words, "grief without faith . . . death without hope." She expresses her appreciation for the pious good wishes of her friends and relatives who were believers, but then renders this judgment: "None of what they said was true. There is no heaven, no door at the end of my life that I will find my boy behind, no paradise. . . . He simply had ceased to exist. . . . If there is something more, it's not something we know. If we can't even grasp how it is that we got here, how can we know with any certainty where, if anywhere, we go when we die?" And then she offers this small consolation: "This is the one comfort that unbelief gives you, that this life will end and the pain you carry along with it."*

I sympathize very much with the writer of this essay. I empathize with her terrible grief—how terrible it is to lose such a young child!—and I admire her intellectual honesty. I also agree with her fundamental point that we cannot know with rational certainty either how we got here nor where, if anywhere, we go when we die. Every human life, regardless of faith or unbelief, is completely shrouded by this cloud of mystery.

But, on the occasion of the death of a loved one, we are not just confronted with the abstract question of what we can know with certainty about how we got here and where we go after we die. We are confronted much more concretely with the question of the ultimate meaning of a particular person's particular human life. What does this

* Amber Scorah, "Surviving the Death of My Son after the Death of My Faith," *New York Times*, May 31, 2019.

person's life mean, in the end, now that the end is here? How does this person's unique life and death fit in with the meaning of everything?

At the end of the day, there are really two basic answers to that question:

One answer presumes that, in the beginning, there is nothing at all. Absolutely nothing. Then, poof! Suddenly there is brute mindless force that we call matter—protons, neutrons, gravity, all that stuff—which somehow inexplicably ends up being fine-tuned to work together to produce the apparent beauty and order all around us. Then, poof again! Matter takes the form of mind. At that point you have consciousness and a human person, who is really ultimately nothing other than the interaction of matter: protons, neutrons, electrons, etc. At some point, the interaction of all this matter begins to malfunction and ceases to produce consciousness and the person disappears forever. Mind goes back to just being matter. In this version of things, the human person is an arbitrary and temporary accident of the random interaction of matter— nothing more. Human persons erupt into existence out of mere matter and they dissolve back into unconscious matter. That's all.

Was that really all that was David Burnett? Was that really the ultimate reality behind all these stories and beautiful testimonials that we shared at the wake last night?

But the other answer to the question of the meaning of a person's life is that human persons are reflections and manifestations of the personal source of all reality. Consciousness does not just magically and inexplicably erupt out of unconscious matter. Rather, consciousness is the very ground and source of reality, the consciousness of a perfectly knowing and perfectly loving and perfectly creative being, who brings forth creation as his artistic work and makes human beings in his own image and likeness so that they may become co-artists with him, co-knowers and co-lovers with him, sharers in his intelligence and love and creativity and the ecstasy of his perfect life.

In the Christian version of this answer, at some primordial point in humanity's earliest hours, human beings rejected this offer of being co-artists with God and co-sharers in the divine life, and decided instead to dedicate themselves to power and consumption, to domination and greed, rather than to knowledge and love and participation in the beauty and ecstasy of divine life. And so death entered into human life, as the natural consequence of the fact that humanity had chosen a dead end for its own existence. But, again according to this Christian version, God could not stand to let his human creatures abide in death. So his final answer to the dysfunction of human beings that led to death was to become a human being himself in order that he himself might die a perfect death, a death suffered with such perfect knowledge and love and forgiveness and immersion into the beauty and ecstasy of divine life that it was a life-giving death, a death that turned death inside out and that resulted in the final affirmation of life: resurrection.

In this version of things, reality is first and finally a love story: it begins with love and ends with love, and the middle is the great reconciliation that recovers lost love and ushers in the eternal reign of love. Indeed, "what wondrous love is this," as we sang in our opening song.

Now, we can have endless and intricate debates as to which of these two versions is more rationally plausible, more intelligible, more fulfilling, and more affirming of the dignity of human life. But that would be beside the point of our present purpose. Our present purpose is not to debate these questions in an abstract way but to consider the witness of David's life. Because, in the end, it matters less which version we say we believe than which version we give witness to in the way we live our lives.

A person who is dedicated to greed and exploitation and domination and boundless consumption and self-assertion at all costs is declaring with their way of life that what they really believe—regardless of what they *say* they believe—is that reality is essentially a matter of brute force and that knowing and loving and creativity and virtue are all arbitrary and temporary accidents that have no ultimate value in themselves. What has value, though only temporarily, is to try to get as many kicks and thrills as possible by manipulating as much as you can the brute force that rules the universe.

This is not how David lived.

David lived his life in such a way as to make it truly credible to say that the human being is the image and likeness of God.

David reflected the creative intelligence of God in the way he was endlessly fascinated with the miracle of how everything worked, how everything was wonderfully and intelligently designed: whether it was the migration patterns of birds or the mechanics of any and every human artifact. The ancient Greeks, and the early Greek Christians, referred to the divine creator as "craftsman" and certainly David was a consummate and ingenious craftsman.

David also reflected divine providence in the way that he was always preoccupied with arranging everything for the benefit of others. His life was a wonderful manifestation of divine benevolence and goodness in the way that he was always so eager to help others. Nothing seemed to please him more or to give him more fulfillment than to help someone else. A few days ago, his wife, Gail, told me simply, "No one has ever told me that David did a bad thing to them." What an extraordinary testament that is to David's way of life. Who of us can be confident that a similar thing can be said of us by those we leave behind?

Now Gail also mentioned to me in that conversation that, on the other hand, David did not stand up for himself very much. Sometimes, she had to intervene on his behalf, as we heard in one of the stories last night. But, in its own way, that too is a reflection of God. Contrary to the way that people try to manipulate the authority of God by provoking fear and invoking divine anger and vengeance, the Christian revelation of God through Jesus Christ is that God generally does not stand up for himself! The God of Jesus Christ gives people freedom, gives people space to abuse that freedom, lets people abuse him and belittle him, and takes the consequences of people's sins upon himself in exchange for the offer of forgiveness and healing. The God who lets himself be crucified on the cross is a God who clearly does not make it a priority to stand up for himself. Instead, he is a God who chooses to stand up for others, regardless of the cost to himself. David's extraordinary meekness and tireless benevolence gave witness to this God.

All of this is not to say, of course, that David was God. David was a creature who gave a wonderful and powerful witness to the splendor of his Creator, but he was nevertheless a creature. And just like you and me, he was a sinner. St. Paul says, "All have sinned and fallen short of the glory of God." In saying this, St. Paul teaches us that sin is not really, in the end, a matter of breaking some rules that God has arbitrarily stipulated so that we don't have too much fun. In fact, sin is nothing else than falling short of the glory of God. Sin is nothing else than failing to reflect the full glory of God. Which is to say that sin is nothing else than failing to be completely, perfectly, divinely glorious.

Rom. 3:23

That's what God wants us to be, and we all fall short of that ideal, that glorious vision and aspiration that God desperately desires for each and every one of us. But the Christian revelation does not tell us, despite the distortions of many Christians, that God is vengeful and spiteful and wrathful with us because we fall short of his glory. Rather, when we fall short of the glory of his majesty through sin, God shows forth the glory of his mercy through forgiveness.

So, if on the one hand, we are called today to recognize the witness of David's life in reflecting divine glory, we are also called, on the other hand, to commend him to the glory of God's mercy by asking God to forgive him for his sins. In the Byzantine liturgy of Easter, we declare that through the resurrection of Christ, forgiveness has shone from the grave. Indeed, there is no resurrection without forgiveness and Christ's resurrection is the final testimony that God has forgiven us all our sins. And so St. Paul tells us in our reading today: "It is God who acquits us. Who will condemn? It is Christ Jesus who died, rather, was raised . . . who intercedes for us. What, then, will separate us from the love of Christ?" In order to commend David *Rom. 8:34–39* to God's forgiveness, in a truly authentic way and not just superficially, it is important that we too search our hearts and forgive David for any way in which he fell short of the glory of God in his relations toward us. At the same time, of course, we need to ask David's forgiveness, in the silence of our hearts, for the times we failed to manifest the fullness of divine glory in our relation to him.

Dear friends, David has now gone ahead of us in the pilgrimage we are all making to our heavenly homeland, to our Father's house. It is indeed true that none of us can *John 14:2* know with the certainty of experience where we are going, just as none of us has any experiential knowledge of where we came from before we were thrown into this earthly existence. But shrouded in this impenetrable cloud of mystery, we are nevertheless invited today to consider the witness of David's life itself. I personally cannot see that it makes any sense to see David's life as a confluence of mere matter from which mind and soul are now removed forever. It makes much more sense to me to see that David's life came from a divine and supremely loving Person who is now welcoming him back to his eternal home, where he will be filled with the fullness of God's glory and will *Wis. 3:7* "shine and dart about as sparks through stubble." As we continue our own pilgrimage through the stubble of this mortal life, let us rejoice in the luminous witness of David's life and pray that we too will join him one day and revel together with him in the endless festival of light that is our eternal destiny.

We ask this through the Light himself, who came into this world to become the light of the world and to guide this darkened world into the splendor of his divine glory, Jesus Christ our Lord. Amen.

In Communion with
Gary Knoppers

Isaiah 25:6a, 7–9; Psalm 93;
1 Corinthians 15:51–57; John 14:1–6

My sisters and brothers, dearly beloved in the Lord:

When we heard, mere weeks ago, the unspeakably sad news of the passing from this life of our beloved Gary Knoppers, the sting of death pierced into depths of our being of which we are not normally aware. The howls of death's victory cries bellowed in our hearts and mocked the hopes that we had once cherished for Gary's recovery. Grief and devastation crashed over us like mighty waters that lifted up their voice; they lifted up their thunder and left us mute in shock and helplessness.

1 Cor. 15:55

Ps. 93:3–4

Still, we found and continue to find solace in the living memories of Gary's beautiful life that was so full of blessings, gratefully received and graciously given. We shared stories of how Gary had impacted our lives, how lively and

---

This sermon was preached at a Roman Catholic memorial liturgy for my dear friend and colleague, the acclaimed biblical scholar Gary Knoppers.

precious that impact was and is, how incomprehensible that this impact is now sundered from the one who made it.

Speaking for myself, I have known Gary for only a relatively short time. Yet, he made a deep impact on me also, first and foremost by his spirit of welcome. Even though I did not know Gary before coming to South Bend, his gracious welcome of me and my family was a deeply touching realization of the exhortation of the apostle Paul, "Welcome one another, as Christ has welcomed you, for the glory of God." I was even more profoundly impressed and edified by Gary's deep and lifelong welcome of the Word of God, by which he fulfilled another apostolic exhortation to "let the Word of God dwell in you richly, teaching and admonishing one another in all wisdom . . . with thankfulness in your hearts to God." Gary's welcome of the Word of God was manifest especially in his reveling in God's concrete and material involvement in this world, in time and space. His faith delighted in the very tangible and palpable signs of God's covenantal love: the people of Israel and their historical journey; the city of Jerusalem; and the liturgical celebration of the sacraments, especially his life-long exultation in the sacrament of marriage to his wife, Laura, and the beautiful fruits of that marriage, David and Teres.

Rom. 15:7

Col. 3:16

One consequence of Gary's steadfast and imperturbably solid grounding in the Word of God is the impression that he seemed to emanate of being unshakeable, a walking demonstration of the words of the psalmist: "The righteous will never be moved; he will be remembered forever. . . . his heart is firm, trusting in the Lord." Yet, Gary was also easily moved by the plight of others. When numerous people were praying for him in what were to be his last days, he asked that people also pray for the people of Africa and Yemen.

Ps. 112

All of us here can tell our own stories and find in these remembrances some solace from our shock and grief. Yet, we keep coming back to the sheer bitterness of the still incomprehensibly terrible fact that Gary is not here. Tossing and turning in our wounded spirits, we can shift from remembrance of the past to hope for the future. In the midst of our anguish, our faith gives us potent consolation, reminding us that, for Gary, life has not ended, but changed, that his soul is now safe with the Lord, and that, one day, when the trumpet will sound, his body will be raised incorruptible and immortal. But even if faith reassures us that Gary has been welcomed into the Lord's embrace, and even if hope beckons us to look forward to our reunion with him when our own earthly pilgrimage is consummated, still our love insists that we must be with Gary now. We, who love Gary, want to be with him now. It is not enough for us just to remember him as he was, or to look forward to meeting him in the distant future. We want to be with him now.

1 Cor. 15:52–54

My brothers and sisters, this is the real challenge of our faith and hope and love in the Lord Jesus Christ: that we be open to receive the gift that our risen Lord offers us, which is to be with Gary now. We can be assured that this is the gift that the Lord offers us, because if it is true, as the apostle Paul says, that Jesus is not Yes and No but always Yes, then Jesus is not just Yes in the past and the future, but Yes now also. Jesus, our crucified and risen Lord, in whom "every one of God's promises is a Yes," the Vanquisher of death and the Lord of life, is the faithful Yes to our desire to be with Gary now.

2 Cor. 1:19

2 Cor. 1:20

Just as we do not have to wait until we see the glorified risen body of the Lord in the flesh in order to be with him, but we rejoice in our communion with him now, so we do not have to wait until the sounding of the last trumpet in order to be with Gary again. Even now, we can again find joy in our communion with him, even in the midst of our grief. We can be assured about this because we know that Christ the Head is never separated from his members. Whenever we have communion with Christ, we have the opportunity to be in communion with all his members.

From the perspective of our broken world, full of divisions and separations, the ultimate separation and division is between those who are alive in this world and those who have died and are no longer visibly present. But it is not so for us. We believe, as Christians, that Christ has broken down this final wall of division just as he has broken down *Eph. 2:14* every other wall. Just as in Christ, there is no longer the separation of the chosen and the not-chosen, the slave and the free, the male and the female, but all are one in Christ Jesus, so there is no longer, in Christ, the separation of the living and the dead. Those of us who are alive on this earth have already died with Christ. We were baptized into his death and now always carry the death of Jesus in our body, so that the life of Jesus may also be manifest in our *2 Cor. 4:10* bodies. At the same time, those who seem, in the eyes of the world, to have simply died now live in Christ, certainly no less than they did while they walked on this earth. But if they live in Christ, they are also present whenever Christ is present, and we can have communion with them through our communion with Christ.

Therefore, in faith, we know that we still have a living communion with our beloved Gary, a communion whose deepest content is our sharing together in Christ's death and resurrection. As we carry the death of Jesus in our body so that the life of Jesus may be manifest in our bodies, we also carry the death of our beloved Gary Knoppers in ourselves, in the body of the church, so that the enduring life of Gary in Christ may also be manifest in us. And just as whenever we eat the bread and drink the cup of the Lord's presence, we proclaim the Lord's death, we also proclaim *1 Cor. 11:26* Gary Knoppers's death in the Lord. And just as we have already risen to newness of life through the resurrection of the Lord, so Gary is still our companion and fellow-sharer *Rom. 6:4* in this newness of life, even while he waits in the bosom of Abraham for the universal resurrection of all flesh.

Of course, it is true that our communion with Gary has now changed, even if it is not ended. It is true that we can no longer have communion with Gary merely according to the flesh, and because of this our hearts are troubled, and full of sorrow. But in this sorrow, our faith challenges *John 16:6* us to accept the passing over, the Passover, of Gary from this world, as not only a loss for us (though it will always be that, as long as we are still on pilgrimage in this mortal world), but also as one of the firstfruits of the universal Passover from the old creation to the new. St. Paul gives us a glimpse of this mystery when he says:

> From now on therefore, we regard no one according to the flesh. Even though we once knew Christ according to the flesh, we do not know him any longer in that way. If anyone is in Christ, there is a new creation. Every-thing old has passed away; see, everything is new. All *2 Cor. 5:16–20* this is from God, who reconciled us to himself, through Christ, and has given us the ministry of reconcilia-tion. . . . So, we are ambassadors for Christ, since God is making his appeal through us; we entreat you on behalf of Christ, be reconciled to God.

Indeed, throughout his life, Gary was an ambassador for Christ. But even now, though we can no longer know Gary according to the flesh, he is still an ambassador for

Christ. God is still making his appeal through him to us and God is still inviting us to persevere in our communion with Gary, so that we may give heed to this appeal. Through our communion in Gary's life and earthly death, Christ continues to make his appeal to us: "Be reconciled to God. Be reconciled to God, despite your sorrow and grief. Be reconciled to the joy of the resurrection, despite the bitterness of death. Be reconciled to the Passover from the old creation to the new, in which Gary has gone before you to the place that the Lord has prepared for him."

Throughout his life, Gary was a gifted teacher and a true shepherd. Our Christian faith assures us that Gary can still be our teacher and our shepherd through the communion we have with him in the risen Lord and in the Spirit. Among the many precious and life-giving lessons that we can learn through our communion in the life and earthly death of our beloved Gary is a true understanding of the fullness of Christian joy. In his earthly life, Gary taught us that a part of Christian joy is a chaste delight in the concrete material and temporal delights of this earth: friendship, music, a summer barbecue, hockey, walking the dog with his beloved wife. But Gary also taught us throughout his life that Christian joy, in this world, comes above all from welcoming the Word of God, letting it dwell in us richly, celebrating always the wonderful deeds of the Lord by which he daily works salvation in the midst of the earth.

Col. 3:16

Ps. 9:1

Ps. 74:12

Now, through his earthly death, Gary is teaching us to orient our lives more fully toward the consummation of Christian joy, which can only come about through the final exodus from this old creation and the Passover into the new. Gary has now gone ahead of us, as our forerunner, in this final Passover. He has gone to the place that the Lord has prepared for him in the Father's house and, as a faithful servant and ambassador of the Lord, he has gone to prepare with the Lord our places in the Father's house.

John 14:2

Through our love for Gary—a love still very much alive—our hearts are stretched beyond the confines of this constricted existence. In our communion with Gary's death, our hearts are already passing over with him to the new creation that has been inaugurated by Christ's victory over death. So, despite all our sorrow, we have every reason to lift up our hearts and lift up our voices as we cry out: O death, where is your sting? O death, where is your victory? Rejoice, the Lord is King, robed in majesty, enthroned over the waters of death and chaos.

1 Cor. 15:55
Ps. 93:1

My brothers and sisters, as we approach the table of the holy Eucharist, whether to partake of it or to venerate it, our faith assures us that our brother Gary is now present with us, within the living body of the church, which is the body of the risen Lord. Let us now continue our celebration of the rich feast of the Lord's love and his victory over death. Let us also respond to the entreaty of the Lord, which he now proclaims to us through his faithful servant Gary, to be reconciled to him and to the cruciform joy of his kingdom. Let us allow him to wipe away all our tears and to mix them with the chalice of his blood, through which we have communion in the Lord's death and resurrection, and through which also we have a living communion, without interruption, with our beloved Gary Knoppers.

Rev. 21:4

May perpetual light shine upon our beloved Gary, even the eternal radiance of the Father's glory, which the Spirit unfailingly grants to all those who, like Gary, welcome it with joy and thanksgiving. Amen.

Heb. 1:3

WEDDING HOMILY

THE VOICE OF
THE BRIDEGROOM AND
THE VOICE OF THE BRIDE

Ephesians 5:20–33; John 2:1–11

My brothers and sisters who are dearly beloved in Christ
Jesus our Lord:

When the people of Israel had broken God's covenant,
and were overrun by their enemies, and sent into exile
and living in desolation, the prophet Jeremiah announced
a new covenant, whose grace endures among us to this
day. Proclaiming this new covenant, the prophet says:

> "The days are surely coming," says the Lord, "when I
> will make a new covenant with the house of Israel and
> the house of Judah. It will not be like the covenant that
> I made with their ancestors when I took them by the
> hand to bring them out of the land of Egypt—a cov-
> enant that they broke, though I was their husband, says

This homily was preached at the wedding liturgy for Michael and Emma
Shakour, celebrated at the University of Notre Dame on May 29, 2021.

Jer. 31:31–33 the Lord. But this is the covenant that I will make with [them]: I will put my law within them and I will write it on their hearts and I will be their God and they will be my people."

The prophet Jeremiah then continues to describe the consolation and joy of God's new covenant. Speaking in the name of the Lord, he says:

Jer. 33:6–11 "I am going to bring recovery and healing; I will heal them and reveal to them abundance of prosperity and security. . . . And this city shall be to me a name of joy, a praise and a glory . . . in the towns of Judah and the streets of Jerusalem that are desolate . . . there shall once more be heard the voice of joy, and the voice of gladness, the voice of the bridegroom and the voice of the bride, the voices of those who sing as they bring thank offerings to the house of the Lord."

My brothers and sisters, this Scripture is now being fulfilled as we celebrate together the union in Christ, through the sacrament of marriage, of Michael and Emma. We have come together from all parts of this country and even from the cities and towns of Judah and Palestine.* We join together in prayer and celebration after suffering through the devastation of a terrible pandemic and, for some of us, after enduring another eruption of terrible violence in God's holy land, once again desecrated by war and injustice. Yet, in the greatness of the Lord's generous mercy, he has seen fit to lift up our weary spirits today and

---

* Michael is an American of Palestinian origin and many of his Palestinian relatives traveled to Notre Dame to attend the wedding. The homily makes reference to the violent clashes that erupted between Arab and Jewish Israelis in May 2021.

to make us hear the voice of joy and the voice of gladness, the voice of the bridegroom and the voice of the bride.

When people suffer, they look for relief. When we are sad and discouraged, we try to escape from our problems by some kind of distraction. When we are overwhelmed by negativity, we can try to focus on something positive. Of course, two people getting married is a very positive thing. But, today, we celebrate the marriage of Michael and Emma not just because we are happy for the two of them, and not just because we want to distract ourselves and escape from the world's problems, but because Michael and Emma *are* the answer to the world's problems.

Of course, they are not the answer to all the world's problems all by themselves. But they are the answer to the world's problems as representatives and ambassadors of the kingdom of God, which is the complete answer to all the world's problems. Michael and Emma have come here today, seeking to seal their union in the sacrament of marriage, because they want their life together to be a representation and a living witness to God's kingdom. They want the covenant between them to be a living witness to the new covenant that God has made with his church by sending his only begotten Son to live among us and to die for our sins and to be raised for our justification and to pour out his Spirit for our sanctification. *Rom. 4:25*

In coming here today and seeking to seal their union in the sacrament of marriage, Michael and Emma are declaring that a merely natural marriage is not good enough for them. They want a supernatural marriage, a marriage that is full of the power and grace of the kingdom of God and of the new covenant, a marriage that is a representation and a living witness of the marriage of Christ and the church.

A merely natural marriage is a very good and positive thing. It can provide companionship and mutual comfort to the spouses; it can bring forth and nurture children; it can be the basis for a solidarity in good works in the community on the part of the spouses. But a supernatural and sacramental marriage includes all these goods of natural marriage while going far beyond them. A sacramental and supernatural marriage is a living icon of the kingdom of God, where God the Father shares the life of his only begotten Son with us and pours out on us his own Holy Spirit.

A good natural marriage can certainly make a difference for the good of the world. But a sacramental marriage, when the spouses are faithful in receiving the gifts of the sacrament, makes all the difference in the world. A sacramental marriage bridges the distance between a fallen and broken world and the kingdom of God. It is itself the bridge between this fallen world and the kingdom of God, a bridge on which not only the spouses and their children but everyone who comes into contact with them can cross over into the kingdom of God.

The natural goods of marriage, like all the goods of nature, tend to decline over time. Physical attraction can diminish; companionship can become strained by selfishness and other vices; people can become bored with each other. These natural goods are like the wine that ends up running out at the wedding in Cana. In our society, when the wine of the natural goods of marriage runs out, many people—perhaps most—opt for divorce. Others decide to put up with just drinking water instead of wine, settling for a humdrum existence in which the original joy and gladness of the marriage is gone. Far too few couples, even Christian couples, know what it is like to really drink the good wine of the special graces that flow from a sacramental marriage. This is the good wine that the steward in the gospel calls "the best wine," and it comes only when the couple invite Jesus, and the power of his kingdom, into their marriage.

Michael and Emma are wisely not waiting for the good wine of natural marriage to run out before inviting Jesus into their marriage. And they seem to have no intention of just making do with the mere water of a humdrum, unremarkable existence. They have come here seeking the sacrament of marriage because they want the best wine right from the start—the wine of the new covenant and the kingdom of God, the wine that comes from the marriage feast of Christ and the church.

In the reading of today's gospel, Michael and Emma are invited to drink from the best wine of sacramental marriage. In the epistle reading, they are instructed on how this best wine should determine their relations to one another. I know that this is a controversial text and it is easily misinterpreted. When it says that the wife should be subject to her husband, that certainly does not mean that the husband can boss around the wife. The key sentence is the one in which the idea of subjection is first raised, which says, "Be subject to one another out of reverence for Christ." So, the main point is mutual subjection, not *Eph. 5:21* the unilateral subjection of the wife to the husband. Mutual subjection entails a reciprocity of sacrificial love, a love that is not selfish but sacrifices one's own self for the other. This is the love whereby Christ himself subjected himself to the church and emptied himself for her sake, and became her servant, as St. Paul tells us:

> Let each of you look not to your own interests but to the interests of the other. Let the same mind be in you that was in Christ Jesus, who, though he was in the form of God, did not regard equality with God something to be grasped, but emptied himself, taking the form of a ser-

Phil. 2:4–8

vant, being born in human likeness. And being found in human form, he humbled himself and became obedient to death—even death on the cross.

This sacrificial love that Jesus extends to the church is a reflection and an extension of the supreme love of the persons of the Holy Trinity. In speaking of this sublime mystery, St. Gregory of Nazianzus tells us that each of the divine persons is united with the other as much as with himself.* This is what all love strives for—that perfect unity in which union with the beloved is not any less than unity within oneself. But this love is only fully achieved in the persons of the Holy Trinity.

It is precisely because human love is in its very nature ordained to reflect the love of the Holy Trinity that the church considers human love to be sacred. That is also why the church considers the union between a man and a woman to be supremely sacred. Through this union, the two become one flesh and one spirit. Each is ordered to unity with the other as much as each is united to self. Each subjects the self to the other in sacrificial love, and in this way the married couple become a living icon of God's love for the world and of Christ's marriage to the church, and even of the love shared by the persons of the Holy Trinity. This is the love that saves the world and it is the grace of this saving love that Michael and Emma ask for today. They ask it for themselves and for their future children and they ask it for the sake of the salvation of all the world.

My brothers and sisters, after suffering and enduring many troubles in recent times, we now rejoice in this request that Michael and Emma make to Almighty God and we rejoice in our confidence that our good and merciful

* *Oration* 31.16.

God will certainly grant them this request. And so we can give ourselves full permission today to be filled with joy and gladness as we hear among us the voice of the bridegroom and the voice of the bride. Our joy is perfected today because we hear the voice of the bridegroom, Michael, blended into the voice of the bridegroom of the church, Jesus Christ. And we hear the voice of the bride, Emma, blended with the voice of the bride of Jesus Christ, who is the church.

We rejoice all together, with Christ in our midst, and in communion with the whole church, because we know that the voices of Michael and Emma, when blended with the voices of Christ and the church, will sing a song of salvation that will resound throughout the world, from this moment to all eternity. Their whole lives will be that song, a song that sings of God's love and peace, of God's healing and forgiveness, a song of praise and glory to our great, almighty, and all-loving God, the Father, the Son, and the Holy Spirit. Amen.

Index of Scripture

Page references in boldface indicate a sermon on the text